STAND UP AND PREACH

STAND UP AND PREACH

A FORMULA FOR BETTER PREACHING

By

AMBROSE MOODY BAILEY, D.D.

Author of "Evangelism In a Changing World"

ROUND TABLE PRESS, INC.

NEW YORK 1937

PRINTED IN THE UNITED STATES OF AMERICA
BY CORNWALL PRESS, INC., CORNWALL, N. Y.

Dedicated to
The only man in the Church
who has no pastor
and to
The only woman in the Church
who can justly judge his sermons

PREFACE

book is a testimony of joy. Except for the call of God a minister of the Gospel would have lived, like Terah, petty objective, would have directed his energies toward l accomplishments and would never have been challenged the expansiveness of the work of the Christian Church and by the transcendent love of his Lord and Saviour for all mankind. It gave to Terah's son, Abraham, strength and an expanding vision. It makes the preacher victorious over physical handicaps, mental incapabilities and spiritual foes.

This book is a testimony of confident faith in the Christian Church and in the power of the ministry even in this day when so many wish for or expect the defeat of the Christian forces. Its title was inspired from reading Ezekiel 2:1.

Back of its pages is an active love, much prayer, sympathy and an appreciation of the man of God. Often he is lonely, poorly paid, disheartened, craving counsel, dismayed by overwhelming obstacles, but keeping on steadily only because he knows that he is God's man—God-called, God-placed, and to be God-rewarded.

This book is offered in great humility. The experiences of an active ministry are presented, not for personal gratification but for the hope that in sharing our observations and our convictions we can be more faithful in the opportunities for service which overwhelm us by their urgency.

AMBROSE MOODY BAILEY.

Lowell, Mass.

CONTENTS

CHAPTER		PAGE
I.	A City Set on a Hill Cannot Be Hid	1
II.	The Greeks Explained It Thus	12
III.	I Have Chosen You	26
IV.	The Congregation Molds the Preacher	40
V.	Jesus Said It Thus	57
VI.	Effectiveness in Presenting the Christian Message	64
VII.	Have Thy Tools Ready; God Will Find the Work	81
VIII.	On What Shall I Preach?	98
IX.	Preach on the Christian Home	120
X.	Preach Missions	124

CHAPTER I

A CITY SET ON A HILL CANNOT BE HID

Dr. Frederick S. Fleming, the rector of Trinity Parish, New York City, was speaking. The occasion was his annual financial report for 1936.

"I seriously believe the Christian Church would once again bring salvation to the world, and begin to save its own soul, if it had the wisdom and courage to declare a moratorium on preaching for a period of one or two years.

"Why cannot a Christian be permitted to go to church to worship his God without always being assailed by a barrage from the pulpit? There is practically no preaching worthy of the name. Frankly, a moratorium would be a godsend, heartily hailed on both sides by the pulpit and by the pew.

"Sermons without end are being delivered, but there is little preaching. Look for a moment at the subjects of these sermons. For the most part, sermons today are a very poor edition of 'topical' homilectics, a brand of religious 'pep-talks,' sailing forth for a transitory popularity under the guise of being inspirational. Truly the miracle of the Church is the patience of the laity.

"People should speak when they have something to say. May we pray to be delivered from any more preaching campaigns calculated to arouse a benumbed and harassed people who have been preached to death. Bishops' crusades, united preaching missions, city-wide drives, the importation of noted orators—these are samples of the inflictions that advertise their own delinquency.

"We are plagued by a spirit of aimlessness. The Gospel of Christ for us has lost its sureness, its courage, its authority. Where does the weakness lie? The rapid widening of the area of modern living, with its mobility and rapidity of change, new forms of entertainment, the disastrous growth of week end vacations which introduces a new situation that is not so much ungodly as it is shamefully Godless, the disappearance of a home-life and the more insistent encroachment of business upon the hours of those employed, the nervous tension under which we all live, the enormous change in the population of our urban communities; these are among the contributing elements of this problem. Their influence is far-reaching and they must be reckoned with in a reasoned appraisal of the ineffectivenes of a large section of American Christianity."

The Associated Press flashed that news to every newspaper in its service, from Abbeville, Alabama, the first town named in the Atlas, to Yellowstone, Wyoming, the last, and then the cables carried it around the world. The newspapers of the world carried the story as news of interest to their readers.

What makes that utterance so important as a news item? Is it because the Trinity Parish has $32,000,000 worth of taxable property in downtown New York? Is it that its income in 1935 was $2,457,780? Or was it that Trinity Parish sustains eight churches, and gives generously to all general causes of the Episcopal Church? Or was it because this is probably the richest Church Foundation in the world? Or was it because it was a new idea? No! Rev. Bernard Clausen, a Baptist clergyman of Pittsburgh, said before the Northern Baptist Convention in Washington, D.C., in 1935, "Preaching is doomed." *His* words, too, were discussed, it is safe to say, in eight thousand Baptist meeting houses.

The one reason for such news interest in this statement was that the preacher continually is news. Dr. Fleming didn't say that he will stop preaching. He didn't say that he will tell his eight assistants to stop preaching. There is much he didn't say. But what he did say constituted news. It was news because he was a preacher.

The minister of the gospel may not seem important to himself, to his wife, or to his congregation, but he is significant to those who evaluate the passing scene. They look at his barometric reading for the social weather and for the religious conscience of the people. The way he thinks is of interest to the movie showman, the politician, the investor and the historian. Even the large employer of labor is keenly interested in his attitudes.

Human life needs six basic functions; the parent, the producer, the physician or healer, the pedagogue or teacher, the potentate or ruler, and the preacher or spiritual guide. Like the teacher, the preacher gives vision, develops moral stamina and arouses new hope for a better future.

OUR SALARIES ARE NEWS

Our salaries are always news. In the spring of 1922, an old minister was trying to adjust himself and his manner of living to a retirement basis. The parsonage in which he had spent thirty-eight of the fifty-two years of his efficient ministry was now his for life, but his salary income had ceased. Both he and his wife had been ill, a big winter's coal bill was unpaid, and his resources were principally the $25.00 a month pension of the Church. The outlook seemed dark, but confident that the Lord would provide he told his wife that he "still had two hands and a brain."

One day in April a woman reporter of the *New York World* learned that the retired preacher had a horse which was remarkably old and she saw a news story in it. She called, and found an even greater human interest story than she had expected: the horse was exceptionally old—older than any horse had ever been known to live. The preacher had driven him for over thirty-five years, and he had been past fifteen when the preacher had bought him. He had been a race horse of blooded stock. His pedigree and the date of his birth were a matter of record; but while the clerical owner was willing to give all the facts concerning the horse, he would not give the facts concerning himself, and the "story" was crowded into an inch on the first page of the regular edition.

Short as the story was, it immediately attracted attention all over the country. Horse lovers and scientific veterinarians began to investigate. They established the fact that Clover was older than any horse ever known. Letters began to pour in from every state in the Union and from many foreign countries, many of them enclosing gifts for the support of the horse. One was received from Mrs. Harding, the wife of the President, enclosing $100. The Jockey Club of New York offered a pension of $25.00 a month to provide for Clover the remainder of his life—the same amount that his master received from the church after fifty-two years of faithful service.

Not so long after the publicity began, the preacher was asked to loan Clover for a benefit in Madison Square Garden. A padded car was sent for the horse, with an attendant and veterinarian to look after him. The preacher and his wife were the guests of the projectors of the benefit for a wonderful week. The publicity he received opened undreamed of avenues for service. In one month he preached eight times and traveled eight hundred miles. The striking interest aroused by the old horse became the text for editorials everywhere, drawing contrasts between the public concern for an old horse and the general concern for the ministers who have given their lives for the preaching of religious truth.

Babson's figures for ten years ago, even before the depression, if reported correctly, showed 180,000 ministers in the United States of whom one per cent. received $4,000 or more per year. Three per cent. received less than $3,000; ten per cent., $2,000; ten per cent., $1,500; sixty-six per cent., $1,000; and ten per cent., less than $500. At about the same time a major denomination in Minnesota announced that the average salary of their clergy was $2.61 per day. Bakers were reported as receiving $2.81; blacksmiths, $2.72; brick layers, $5.47; painters, $3.45; plumbers, $4.43; stone masons, $4.58; linotype operators, $5.28. The average wage of men in these trades was $1,200 per year; seventy per cent. of the preachers received $1,000 or less.

OUR SONS ARE NEWS

Our sons are news. "If a man bites a dog that's news" runs the adage. The unusual is news. Most of our sons are good men. That is why a bad one makes the headlines. Woodrow Wilson and Charles Evans Hughes came from the parsonage. So did President Arthur and Grover Cleveland. And so did Henry Clay. Six of the signers of the Declaration of Independence were sons of clergymen. Ministers' sons have often graced the pages of literature, as is shown by the names of Bancroft, Emerson, Holmes, Lowell, Mitchell, Norton, and Parkman. In the field of science is Agassiz and S. F. B. Morse. Among the great families of America all beginning in a minister's home are the Mathers, the Edwards, Fields, Beechers, Everetts, Wares, Alexanders, Hopkins, Waylands, Judsons, Boardmans, Dwights. In the *Cyclopedia of American Biography* are listed 1,270 names of eminent men who were the sons of clergymen. There are 510 sons of lawyers, and 350 sons of physicians. Of the names in the National Hall of Fame twenty are from ministers' homes, and among these, Jonathan Edwards, William Ellery Channing, Emerson, Holmes, Clay, Agassiz, Bancroft, Beecher, Stowe, Lowell, Phillips Brooks. The wives of five presidents were ministers' daughters—Mrs. John Adams, Mrs. Millard Fillmore, Mrs. Franklin Pierce, Mrs. Benjamin Harrison, and the first Mrs. Wilson.

PEOPLE WRITE BOOKS ABOUT US

Books written about us have become news. I am not speaking of the great biographies such as Alexander V. G. Allen's *Phillips Brooks* or Gamaliel Bradford's tours de luxe. Enter any library. We put out our hand blindly and touch brave Charlotte Bronte carrying on in her father's parsonage; or we pick up Laurence Sterne's *Sentimental Journey* or *Tristram Shandy*. We sample his sermons to find them glowing with phosphorescent brilliance, devoid of heat. We reach toward the fiction stack, and our fingers touch Harold Bell Wright, once a minister himself, in *The Calling of Dan Matthews;* S. R. Crockett, friend of Stevenson, in *The Sticket Minister;* Ralph Connors' *Sky Pilot;* J. M. Barrie's *The Little Minister;* John Watson's (Ian MacLaren) *The Bonnie Brier Bush;* Winston Churchill's *The Inside of the Cup;* Jane Austen's *Pride and Prejudice,* the story of a minister's marriageable daughters; Sinclair Lewis, without creed or code, gaily thumbing his nose at us in *Elmer Gantry;* Voltaire, noblest cynic of them all, and with the most reason, in *Candide,* and so on and on, not forgetting dear Oliver Goldsmith in his *The Vicar of Wakefield.* And even so we have not turned to the playwrights. Here is Channing Pollock. Every play from his pen is a sermon, every actor a most eloquent and artistic preacher. And there is Charles Rand Kennedy in the *Servant in the House,* and most recent of all, this last winter's stage success, *And So Goodbye,* starring Phillip Merrivale.

WE MAKE HEADLINES

Our social utterances and our moral lapses have been news. Volume nineteen of *Who's Who in America* for 1936-1937 contains 29,128 names. Of these 2,817, or nearly ten per cent. of the whole, are clergymen. That is not news. But let one of these fall from his perilous height and the world reads about it.

We have no difficulty in making the headlines. All we have to do is to marry or refuse to marry an ex-king or a Reno graduate; or denounce, or refuse to denounce, national drunkenness; or inveigh against, or enlist in, the stupidity of war; or refer to our neglect of the alien; or give Mussolini or Hitler a castigation; or lament the mobbing of a negro; or plead for a greater tolerance among the races and the creeds. These are almost "sure fire" recipes for making the front page. If these fail, denounce the greed of a few chosen capitalists, or advocate unregulated rugged individualism.

UNEXPECTED NEWS

There are other features of our task that are even more important and which in due time, let us pray, will be recognized as news. Here is a single authentic instance. A tradesman owned a large store and was posssessed of a magnetic personality, but the credit men watched him closely because he was drinking heavily and gambling carelessly. Then came a day when he accepted Christ. His habits changed. Today he has a business of which the whole community is proud. That preacher who changed his life was not a non-producer. He produced business. He cemented the home. He promoted self-respect in the entire community. That was news of the type that should have the headlines.

Here is another case of a boy who changed completely from a loafer in a village pool room to a college graduate. He says of himself that if the preacher had not found him when he did, he would have cost the state a goodly sum in the reformatory.

A late biography affirms that one of our great leaders was in childhood possessed of a mischievous bent. He organized a band of adolescent boys to remove nuts and bolts from railway cars and farmers' wagons, just for fun. But Christ saved him. There is not one in a thousand who would believe that story possible if coupled with the name to which it belongs. Did the preacher in that case produce nothing of value?

MORE THAN NEWS

It is the preacher's greatest glory that we are seers for the race. One of the powerful groups of the sculptor Lorado Taft is entitled "The Blind." The figures are from an almshouse and all are either insane or blind except one—a child. Twilight has come on and they are lost. A blind mother has hoisted this child—her sane and seeing little one—to her shoulder, and the child affords the vision to bring the helpless multitude to safety. In like manner we try to lead others to see the way to God. What news stories could be told of this phase of our every day task!

In the spring of 1921, one of the most severe storms in the history of the Pacific Northwest blew across the Olympic peninsula. For forty miles the traveler might traverse a road along which, on either side, to a total depth of thirty miles the storm had wrought destruction. Eleven billion feet of timber, fir, spruce, cedar, and hemlock fell. Great trees ten feet in diameter and three hundred feet in height, and that had been growing for two hundred and fifty years came down in horrible profusion. There was but one thing that man could do. Mills could not be built to salvage the lumber for there were no railroads to bring it out. The situation was a fire hazard to all industry in the region, and a menace to every human habitation in the territory. The state set up vigilant supervision with great patience, while God reconstructed that which had been destroyed. And now, after these years, nature herself has accomplished the beginnings of reforestation. Much of our work as servants of God is like that in the field of supervision. We watch as those who shall give an account. We are the watchman on the mountain top, the overseers, the episcopi.

Let us remember, too, the oft repeated story from Eusebius, the historian, of John the aged at Ephesus. He returned from a long absence to inquire of the curate in whose care the church had been left, as to the whereabouts of a young mountaineer whom he had baptized.

"He has gone back to his old associates and is a robber once more," was the report. The old man mounted his ass, and wended his way into the defiles and passes of the hill country until he reached robber territory, where he was captured. When he was taken before the chieftain, he found, as he had expected, that the head of the band was his lost convert.

May the greatest piece of news told concerning us be that we bear the good news that changes the lives and habits of men.

Here is the way Victor Hugo put it in his immortal story:

"Come in," said the bishop.

"I am a convict, do you hear, my name is Jean Valjean!"

"Madam," said the bishop, "you will put clean sheets on the bed. Sit down, sir, and warm yourself. We shall sup directly."

* * *

"Jean Valjean, my brother, you no longer belong to evil but to good. I have bought your soul of you. I withdraw it from black thoughts and the spirit of perdition and give it to God."

We preachers in many varied experiences are day by day, week by week, month by month, reclaiming spiritual wastes and giving into the husbandry of our God lives which can yield a hundred, even a thousand fold in spiritual joys and power.

Are we non-producers? No wonder we are news.

CHAPTER II

THE GREEKS EXPLAINED IT THUS

Dr. Frederick Taylor, for more than thirty years pastor of the First Baptist Church of Indianapolis, once said with an engaging smile, "I don't know the difference between a speech and a sermon—do you?" That afternoon there were more Greek Lexicons and more Cruden's Concordances consulted than had been opened in a year.

When a first-century Christian heard the word "preacher," the picture that formed in his mind was of the king's servant driving into the public square. The trumpets sounded. The people came to respectful attention. The herald, in colorful livery which advertised his function, stood up and delivered his message. He announced either that the king was at the gate, and demanded the loyal obeisance of his subjects, or that he, the king's representative, had a message from the king to which all men were to listen. It was not his message: it was the king's. He received it and he delivered it unchanged. He was a voice. This spectacle was the one seized upon by the early church to describe the position and function of its minister. The Greek word which describes this is κήρυξ (karux), a messenger or herald.

If the first-century preacher did not preach after this fashion his congregation knew that something was lacking.

The English words for preacher and preaching are listed 119 times in the concordance. The word κήρυξ is foremost of all. It comes from the more ancient word, γῆρυς (gárus), a voice.

John the Baptist was literal in describing his task when he said, "I am the *voice* of one crying in the wilderness." The message he shouted to the winds and to the hearts of men was what he was given of God. It was this that kept him calm and fearless when he stood before Herod and said: "It is not lawful for thee to have her."

THE PREACHER IS A HERALD

The business of preaching is lifted above the secular. It is the delivery of an authentic word from God. Preaching is a divine function performed through a human agent. When an eternal message is wedded to a faithful human voice, that is preaching. The preacher who makes that discovery is like Columbus when his lookout shouted, "Land!" Before him opens a new continent of possibilities.

Dr. George A. Gordon was right when he said that in an entire lifetime he had not known five ministers of questionable character. But ministers, of all men, abhor the odor of sanctity. They are honest, God-fearing men. And they do not wish to be reminded of it. To say to such, "you are heralds and representatives" seems at first blush to be unctious. Yet this is what has always been meant when we insist that there is a sense in which the minister is in an historic succession. We do not refer to an historic hand laid upon us, setting us apart, but to an historic voice which we hear and whose message we repeat. This sets us apart.

Ministers want to live like God but they ask for no halo. They do not want to be called holy any more than a young woman wishes for the description, "she's a nice girl." Yet they cannot escape from being God's chosen men.

Let's go to the "barrel" of sermons we have preached. You and I will have no difficulty in separating the addresses there into two groups. In one group we put those in which we expressed ourselves freely and on all sorts of topics. But in the other group we place those in which we truly listened to a Voice, speaking through us for the salvation of all men.

In one pile there is a gleam of insight that sets them apart. These glimpse the judgment of another world. But in this other, which is far larger, we hear no voice speaking but our own. We have tried our best to interest a congregation for thirty minutes. One group of sermons is divine and one is human in origin. In one group of sermons, God spoke. In the other He did not, or if so, then very faintly. The time-serving voice of scullion secularity can dress itself quite acceptably in the court clothes of orthodoxy, and sometimes fool everyone, even the preacher himself. If one doubts it, let him read John Bunyan's description of Mr. Talkative.

The honest truth is that an address may obey every law of composition, yet be "of the earth, earthy." And it may violate every canon of literary taste, yet be delivered under the aspect of eternity.

Dr. Taylor said, "I don't know the difference between a sermon and a speech." Probably he did not. He did not need to. He was so essentially eternal in outlook that he preached no matter what he said. He spoke once on "Cleaning Up the City Dump," but when he finished we all felt that he had lifted our very souls into the presence of the Master. His preaching was not so much in his choice of texts, but in an aroma of heaven that he carried. He spoke once on the text, "Thy strength is to sit still." When he had concluded, all wished to express our thoughts in the words of Whittier:

"Dear Lord and Father of mankind,
Forgive our feverish ways,
Reclothe us in our rightful mind,
In purer lives thy service find,
In deeper reverence, praise."

The ancient Hebrew when asked what God did all day long, replied that God sat reading the Torah. But John the Evangelist has a better answer: "In the beginning was the Word." What does God do all day long? He speaks to us in Christ. God does not read words all day long. He utters them. He is Himself the Voice.

Once in the New Testament we have this distinction of preaching as the Voice recognized. Turn to I. Cor. 1:18. Our English text of this famous passage reads, "for the preaching of the cross is to them that perish foolishness." Here the Greek is ὅ λογος γὰρ ὅ τοῦ σταυοῦ (ho logos gar ho tou stauroú,)—"the word of the cross."

Preaching is a clearly spoken, understandable word that tells us of the heart of God. The prophets were such preachers. Christ was this eternally. We utter in a sentence what He put into a life and a death. Preaching in this sense has back of it the conviction of all the Old Testament prophets, "thus saith the Lord."

PREACHING IS AUTHORITATIVE

But there is an even stronger word for preaching, κήρυγμα and κηρύσσω pronounced kárugma and karússo. Everywhere that these words are used they mean, "this is said with great authority." These forms are used thirty times in the New Testament. This concept is to preaching what the vein of ore is to the mine. We have all been to church and asked with the Ethiopian eunuch when he addressed the evangelist Philip (Acts 8:34), "of whom speakest the prophet this? of himself, or of some other man?" We have been in services with no more depth than a town meeting, and when it was all over the bewildered spirit has gone away saying, "Jesus I know, and Paul I know, but who are you?"

PREACHING IS THE DECLARATION OF GOOD NEWS

The Greek word for evangelize is translated "preach" thirty-six times. Sometimes it is used in the same sentence interchangeably with the word, "herald," as in Jesus' famous pronouncement at Nazareth in Luke 4:18: "The Spirit of the Lord is upon me because he hath anointed me to evangelize the poor, (that is to give them good tidings) to herald the acceptable year of the Lord." Occasionally the word evangelize or preach has been worked into combination with some prefix like *dia* or *kata* which carries the idea that Paul and the Apostles preached the good news through or carried their task to successful completion. Such a word becomes almost a shout of victory.

The eternal message we declare is essentially one of good news. Of course every emphasis it contains, when considered in and of itself, is not good news. It is not good news that all men are sinners, estranged from God, suffering from a sick will, and bent upon their own unhappy and yet certain destruction. It becomes good news only when we link it with the healing and hope which is the heart of the gospel.

So preaching becomes the announcement of life and health and salvation for man and for the whole human race.

PREACHING IS TO BE DELIVERED IN COMMON SPEECH

In eight well known passages the word for preaching is some form of λαλῆζω as λαλῆσαι or of λαλέω (Acts 16:1). Here preaching was thought of as familiar talk in common speech. We would not be too far afield if we said, "they chatted in pleasant fashion about the gospel." It was out of such chats that Wyclif's Lollards received their name, but in their case the appellation was intended to be derisive. We may receive this hint from another source. St. Francis went out one day with one of his disciples, Brother Leo, to preach. They wandered through the fields conversing naturally with laborers. Bye and bye they returned. "But I thought we were to preach," said the student. "We did," replied Francis. "We preached as we walked and talked with men." The logical conclusion of this bit of insight is to see that all our preaching shuns holy tones and everything artificial. "Jesus opened his mouth and taught them saying—"

PREACHING IS NOT A LENGTHY, FLOWERY, ARGUMENTATIVE DISCOURSE

Only twice the word "preaching" in the New Testament is used to denote a long, formal discourse (διαλέγομαι), and it is worthy of note that in both of these texts it is in connection with the same incident. Paul discoursed in lengthy fashion and Eutychus fell asleep (Acts. 20:7). However, we would be forcing the exegesis altogether too far to infer that one was not to think and prepare carefully for what he had to say. The term discourse probably referred both to the length and to the legal, argumentative style. It was this manner of preaching that he said he had abandoned when he wrote to Corinth. It was a style that failed him utterly on Mars Hill. Canon Farrar says that clearly. People didn't like debate even then. It tends to make one speak with boxing gloves. Read Paul's sermon at Athens and it is clear why this was so. He patronized them. He adorned his message. He wore them out. And finally, rather apologetically, he came to the point. They were polite; they bowed. "We will hear you again," they said. But he had lost his one chance. "Never again," says Paul. "I determined not to know anything among you save Jesus Christ and him crucified." He stopped using all human expedients and concentrated on the main theme. If a man heard him three minutes he got the point.

He ceased trying to be ornate and conciliatory and began to be straight-forward in his preaching. They might not like it, but they knew where he stood and why.

PREACHING HAS AN ETHICAL CONTENT

The word "preaching" has always included the ethical content of the message. That is to say the word "preaching" always included the idea of the proclamation of the necessity of repentance and reformation. Here Jonah became the perfect illustration as cited in Matthew 12:41, Luke 11:32, and Jonah 3:4. But the preacher also announced the necessity of salvation, and the Christian preacher in the New Testament announced that salvation was to be had through Christ. So,

Thayer's Lexicon points out, it was used in I Cor. 1:21; 2:4; 15:14; in Romans 16:25; II Timothy 4:17; and Titus 1:3.

New Testament preaching and Old Testament prophecy are not so different nor so far apart as some would have us think. The Old Testament says, "Cease to do evil, learn to do well." The New Testament recognizes that such moral activity is impossible apart from Christ. The missionary to the Indians said, "You must do unto others as you would be done by." The chief replied, "Teacher, I can't do that, unless someone works a miracle in my heart." He was right. Preaching presupposes that God can help a man do the impossible. Preaching has in it no vainglorious boasting that we are saved by the works of the law. Works are always a fruitage growing on the Tree of Life (Gal. 5:22).

PREACHING IS GRAVE

The word κηρύσσω introduced another idea or made plain what was only implied before. This word for preaching says it must always contain the note of gravity. It is used thirty times in this sense. It was as if the speaker were to say, "the word I now bring you is of the utmost importance. This word must be listened to and obeyed." It is used in the New Testament repeatedly of John the Baptist, of Jesus, of the apostles, of Paul, and of all the Christian teachers. Gravity is not a lack of humor. It is a sense of weightiness, of importance, of command. It says, "Today if ye will hear his voice, harden not your hearts."

There is a place for humor on the lips of an ambassador. Saito of Japan, to give but a single instance, has a most engaging personality. As a raconteur he cannot be excelled.

He has done his country rare service by his unreserved smile. But the danger latent in all humor lies in the barb it carries. The late Dr. John H. Jowett said he had never heard a bit of facetiæ in the form of a story that was not either impure, untrue, or unkind. He would have none of it. Rowland Hill, on the other hand, never preached without it. It must be admitted that the pulpit wag runs many dangers. Cowper said, "Tis pitiful to court a grin, when you should woo a soul." Some will fear his wit as having a personal intent to hurt. Some will come only so long as they can be amused. Some will demand an ever more strongly spiced diet. Some can charm with humor and retain their integrity and their ability to tell the truth with fidelity and conviction. But where one will succeed more will fail. Humor that is natural, occasional, and unforced, and that easily swings into line with one's major purpose is no more to be discarded than it is in general conversation. There is however a marked difference between the bright sparkle of an alert and kindly mind, and the smart banter of the professional entertainer who waits to trip the unwary. The minister will be afraid to hurt and ashamed to lie, and fearful always of the subtle double meanings that carry impurity.

WHAT IS OUR RELATION TO PREACHING?

Our first relation becomes one of obedience. We must follow the new insight or more insight will not come. That is a universal spiritual law. We face an imperative. The fact that preaching is so regarded without exception on every New Testament page, and so continued until well after the Reformation, puts a burden of proof upon any man who would make it less than the authoritative declaration and the authentic word of an accredited ambassador from the King of Heaven. If it is not this, what is it? It is the possession of this quality which puts the minister in the timeless group where Jesus would have his messengers live and move. More than anything else it was this attitude that so angered the Temple authorities. Yet Jesus says, "As my Father hath sent me, even so send I you." "So!" That is a big word. Christianity is an historic and objective revelation. "That which we have heard, which we have seen with our eyes, which we have looked upon, and our hands have handled of the Word of Life" (I John 1:1). So! The preacher did not create the facts. So! He cannot alter them. So! He declares them. So! He is God's prophet. So! The prophet is the "pro-phete," the "speaker for" God. "So send I you!"

Here is one minister who writes that on every Saturday night before he locks the study door, he looks back over his message for the next morning, to see if the raucous noises of an impinging secular world or the static that fills the air has crowded "The Voice" off the air.

How much of my sermon did God give me?

If He were here in the flesh what would he add?

What would he leave out?

Does this exalt Him?

What would He stress? And why?

Who of my tomorrow's congregation needs this message?

Is there power here to change a life?

Am I challenging the faith faculties of the soul? Is this an authentic word?

Did I spin the sermon as a spider spins his web, or did I follow His Design?

Am I an ambassador of the Living God, or do I speak for myself?

He says this method has given him a greater sense of freedom, such as a bird feels when it knows itself to be up-borne. But this does not always follow. Suppose instead one feels fear. Peter should have been happy when freed from prison, "but he wist not that it was true." They still tell the story of the old circuit rider who stood one Sunday morning and said, "Brethren I have no message from the Lord for you today." The country folk are talking of that yet. He lost his pulpit. They thought they could command the prophetic voice. But that isn't the entire story. That was the defense mechanism the old man set up after he was released. The real story was that it was haying time, and the preacher was more anxious to "make hay while the sun shone" than he was to prepare a sermon.

But some will say with fearful heart, "Suppose that should happen to me? What if some week I hear no one speaking?" The question is legitimate. There is a deeper question, even more frightening: "What if I neglect to listen for the Voice?" There is still another frightening question: "What if the message be displeasing to my people?" There is a question even still more disquieting: "Suppose the message make one fanatical and queer?" There is evidence that these are precisely the questions that disturbed the minds of men like Isaiah and Jeremiah and Ezekiel. It is possible for all such to experience a great peace, for our discovery has lifted us far above the canons of taste which are dictated by Mr. Whim or Mrs. Fancy.

Every minister is the victim of certain artificial canons and standards of his day. But the concept that he is an ambassador and representative from heaven releases him from these hampering standards. But it releases him only to put him in bondage to higher, more rigorous bonds. It is as if he were arrested. The Justice of the Peace of the village releases him to the sheriff of the county, the sheriff of the county to the custody of the state, and the state turns him over to the Federal authorities. The highest has him. He becomes like the Roman centurion, a man under authority. He can say to one man, "come," and to another, "go," only because he himself is enlisted under and empowered by the Emperor.

That the message is God's message will not excuse him from hard labor. It will drive him to it, even as the priest of the Temple was required to beat the oil for the light, which derived from the olive trees in the Temple enclosure. Dr. S. Parkes Cadman was once asked what he did to maintain such a high average of pulpit ability and how he kept from slumping. He said, "I fall back upon my knowledge of the English classics." He adorned his message by much study. Harry Emerson Fosdick was asked a similar question. His reported answer was this, "For every one hundred words I speak, I put in one hour of study." E. Stanley Jones, another example of very even performance in the pulpit, who seemingly never has a poor day, has repeatedly said that he spends as long in the silence of prayer immediately before the address as he plans to spend in speaking. All of these men, therefore, make common testimony that the message must have background preparation.

Of course he will have difficulties. Was it Whistler who worked for a week to perfectly picture his mother's hand on canvas, and when he was almost ready to give up in despair, fell on the divan and sobbed like a child, "I can't, I can't"?

He could not because he was aiming at perfection. He could not for the reason that no man can perfectly express anything. Time cannot hold eternity. Of course your people will never appreciate what it cost you.

"But none of the ransomed ever knew,
How deep were the waters crossed,
Nor how dark was the night that the Lord passed through,
Ere He found His sheep that were lost."

The message will come through a personality which has the inherent defects of our age, and our own physical, mental, and social inheritance. This was true of all God's prophets. Our insight and outlook will be human. Paul said, "We have this treasure in earthen vessels." There will be times when concerning certain mundane matters we can only say, "we think we have the mind of Christ." In some cases he must say, "I speak this of permission and not of commandant"; "I have no commandment of the Lord, yet I give my judgment."

Yet there is an authentic word that has been spoken from God, and that still speaks through the pages of Scripture, the person of Jesus, the history of the Church, the crises that face every individual, and the personality of God's ministers regardless of their defects and frailties. It is this sure word that the true prophet and mouthpiece of God seeks. The consciousness that he has such a word gives his calling dignity and his utterance weight. It lifts him out of moods of inferiority, and places him in full view of eternity. When he mounts the pulpit steps he ascends "into the hill of the Lord." When he read the Scripture, he remembers Jerome's happy rendition of Psalm 12:6 "Eloquia Domini, eloquia casta." "The words of the Lord are pure words." Ultimately the lexicon gives one a touch of lightness and joy, that one has not known before. One can afford to smile. A message not one's own! You are compassed about with a great cloud of witnesses, prophets, apostles, martyrs. They watch to see you do your best, to be true, not to a figment of your own imagination but to an eternal message in which you and your Lord are knit as one. If it fails, you and He are both rejected together; if it succeeds, you and He both receive the crown! You are bound up in the bundle of life with Him. "The pleasure of the Lord is prospering in your hand." Does this poem reflect a picture of our preaching?

"He held the Lamp each live-long day
So low that none could miss the way,
And yet so high to bring in sight
That picture fair—of Christ, the Light—
That gazing up—the Lamp between—
The hand that held it was not seen.

He held the Pitcher, stooping low,
To lips of little ones below,
Then raised it to the weary saint
And bade him drink when sick and faint;
They drank; the Pitcher thus between—
The hand that held it scarce was seen.

He blew the Trumpet soft and clear
That trembling sinners need not fear
And then with louder note and bold
To storm the walls of Satan's hold:
The Trumpet coming thus between,
The hand that held it was not seen.

But when our Captain says, 'Well, done,
Thou good and faithful servant! Come!
Lay down the Pitcher and the Lamp,
Lay down the Trumpet—leave the Camp.'
Thy weary hands will then be seen
Clasped in His pierc'd ones, naught between."

CHAPTER III

I HAVE CHOSEN YOU

"My son, John, has been called to preach the gospel." So spoke the sire of yesterday and surprised no one. By this he meant that in some definite supernatural way, God had made known to the youth that preaching and the care of a church was God's wish for his son's life.

So spoke William Carey. Carey's son, Felix, became a missionary and later because of a certain linguistic capability, and because he was on the ground when the need arose, the British nation made of him an ambassador to the Court of Siam. But the father, old William Carey, was never happy about the arrangement in spite of its large stipend. To him, "Felix had driveled into an ambassador." If Carey had been asked, "Is the ministry a call?", he would have quickly answered, "Yes."

So thought Woodrow Wilson. "When I hear some of the things which men say to me by way of putting the arguments to themselves for going into the ministry, I think that they are talking of another profession. Their motive is to do something, when it should be to be something. You do not have to be anything in particular except a kind-hearted man, perhaps, to be a physician; you do not have to be anything nor undergo any strong spiritual change, in order to be a merchant. The only profession which consists in being something is the ministry of our Lord and Saviour—and it does not consist of anything else. It is manifested in other things, but it does not consist of anything else. And that conception of the minister which rubs all the mark of it off and mixes him in the crowd so that you cannot pick him out, is a process of eliminating the ministry itself."

Before this chapter was written letters were sent forty eight preachers, under the seal of confidence,

(1) north, south, east, west; (2) among twelve leading denominations; (3) divided equally among conservative, liberal, and middle of the road groups; (4) old and young.

In this way we thought to get an unbiased answer to the following questions.

1. "When you entered the ministry did you believe yourself called of God?" Forty-six replied, "Yes," one said, "No." One was doubtful.

2. "Do you now regard yourself as a called man?" Forty-eight—"Yes."

3. "Do you believe that those who enter the ministry today should experience a call?" Thirty-seven—"yes"; Eleven—"Yes, but the call needs an explanation."

4. "Would you be willing to tell me the story of your call?" Forty—"yes." Eight—"It would take too long or would be of no consequence."

5. "When the call came, how did it come?" By advice of Sunday-school teacher, 5; by a sense of world needs, 5; by prayer for guidance, 4; by a distinct feeling of God's voice, 4; by a sermon, or at a conference, 4; by advice of pastor, 3; by a sense of man's lost condition, 3; by a dream, 2; by advice of a friend, 1; by reading the Bible, 2; by reading religious book or article, 2; by advice of parents, 1; by a sense of fitness, 1; by a special Providence, 1; by force of circumstances, 1; uncertain, 1.

6. "Was there back of your call a long history of religious instruction in church and family?" Forty-four answered "Yes." Four, no answer.

7. "Was your call different from that which comes to a man in any other occupation?" Thirty-eight—"Yes." Four, "No." Six, "Don't know."

8. "Has your call sustained you in trial?" Forty-eight said "Yes."

In spite of this questionnaire, I continued to have a fear that the concept of the ministry as a divine calling was being overlaid.

Everyone concedes that God has called exceptional men occasionally to be great national leaders—a Washington, Lincoln, Wilson, General Foch, Cromwell. But that God "calls" individuals into his ministry! My fears took me into argument with myself. Everyone uses the expression, and everyone is afraid of it. It is like the cobra safe only in the hands of the charmer. There is no question which we should come to terms with sooner. "Why am I in this profession anyway?"

I attended an ordination service last week. "Were you called of God?" the candidate was asked.

He blushed, stammered, looked as if he were handed a slip by a traffic officer, swallowed, and said, "I beg your pardon?"

The interrogator chosen by the assembly tried to be kind. "Why are you seeking to enter the ministry?"

"Well-er-it's a respectable calling. I think I can do some good."

The moderator smiled encouragingly and he continued,

"My pastor assures me that it is a God-guarded life, a pleasant one, of culture and association with the best people and the best books."

There was an audible smile and one pastor had the grace to blush. The young man was tripping badly now, and the next minute he went sprawling in an ugly fall. "I have always wished for a life of ceaseless variety, with an assured income."

I am merely reporting the conversation and have not intentionally been severe. But the next candidate was almost as bad. He stood nervously adjusting his tie.

"Have you read First and Second Timothy and Titus which are the first books of instruction ever written for the Christian pastoral office?"

A prompt, "Yes sir."

"Have you read the Office of Institution of Ministers?"

"Yes sir."

"Would you care to tell the brethren what the qualities of a good minister are?"

"He should be a man of diligence, sound doctrine, prudence, innocence of life, and compliance with the rules and teachings of his Church. He should tend the flock, not as a man pleaser, but accountable to Christ. He should be able to lead devotions, teach the Word and exercise discipline."

The favorite was off to such a good start that we were not prepared for the spill that he took as he rose to take the barrier.

"Were you called of God to preach?"

He hesitated for an awkward moment, just too long.

"I did not choose the profession for its rewards." He was not going to trip on the hurdle that had thrown his predecessor.

"Then *you* did choose it, did you?"

The interlocutor was giving the candidate his opportunity to state clearly whether this were his choice or whether God had chosen him. The candidate did not fumble. He saw the implications.

"My father drifted into the ministry. He has been happy in it. I was born in the parsonage. Father thinks I cannot do better than to follow in his steps. He can help me considerably I feel sure."

He had shown us his whole heart. He was inheriting the ministry through nepotism. He would be preaching his father's sermons for a lifetime. Perhaps these are rare cases which I have reported but the laity must bear its share of the blame for such a picture. You meet the chairman of the pulpit committee who says, "We have a good pastor *now.*"

"*Good* pastor, what do you mean? You have a good pastor *now?*"

"Well, our other pastor was a good man, I suppose, but he was no mixer."

"You mean this man goes to lodge and attends the service clubs?"

"Yes, that's it, and we call him Bill."

After much reflection I sent another question to the same forty-eight men.

9. "Do you find the idea of a supernatural call to the ministry unpopular today?" Forty-eight—"yes."

10. "Why?" "Because it is seized on by the ignorant and superstitious to recruit the ranks with inferior men," is a fair synopsis of all answers received.

Now we were getting somewhere. The hand that lifted us into the pulpit was not a human hand. But the man so lifted must treat that call with sublime dignity.

A sense of awe will give depth to our preaching that otherwise would be as shallow and storm-tossed as Lake Erie or the English Channel. Of course, not all impressions that come will bear the test of time.

The Cornish miner's wife was calling loudly. "Why don't you answer?" said a passing woman, to children on the street. Quick came the answer,

"Her ain't a callin' we. Us don't belong to she!"

Let us be sure the voice we hear is that of our God. God's call is a personal choice of a certain man to do a certain work. It is not *a* call, but *my* call. The preacher has a "divine right" to such an experience.

Make a case study of the lives of men like Samuel, Isaiah, Ezekiel, or Hosea, to name no more, in the Old Testament; or Paul in the New Testament. Listen to this: "In the year that king Uzziah died I saw also the Lord. . . . And he said, Go and tell this people"; or this, "But the Lord said, to whomsoever I shall send thee, thou shalt go"; or this, "the word of the Lord came expressly unto Ezekiel . . . and he said . . . stand upon thy feet and I will speak unto thee . . . and he said, I send thee"; or this, "Jehovah said to Hosea, Go"; or this, "I was an herdsman . . . and the Lord took me as I followed the flock, and the Lord said . . . 'prophesy unto my people.' "

In the case of Amos the call seems to have come as a conviction of impending national disaster, unless men could be brought into right relation to God. He received his call by a reading of history.

Dr. J. Edgar Park has just reminded us of that famous sentence of Dean Swift in which he says he has "given up all hope for the Church and for Christianity." We are in the mood of that fear right now.

Marcus Dods said more than thirty years ago: "I do not envy those who have to fight the battle of Christianity in the twentieth century." Thoughts like this in Amos' heart instead of driving him from preaching, drove him to it.

Look a moment at calls which come by the advice of parent, minister or friend. Is this legitimate? I think so.

John Rough, pastor of the castle at St. Andrew's, leaned over the pulpit and pointing his finger at a timid young boy, said, "John Knox, God is calling you to preach." In that moment the Scottish Reformation was born and received its baptism. "I charge you that ye refuse not this holy vocation . . . that ye take upon you the public office and charge of preaching."

Some pastors who realize that only they can say all these things adequately, arrange a Youth Sunday when all their youth are most likely to be home from school, and at a special service present these young people with these purposes for signature:

> "Having given my life to Jesus Christ as Savior and Lord, it is my purpose, as the central, controlling aim of my life, to do my utmost to extend the Kingdom of Christ throughout the world.
>
> "I believe that God has a definite plan for my life-work, which it is my purpose to find and to follow, no matter where it may lead me.
>
> "It is my purpose to keep studying the needs of the world and also the plan and will of God as revealed in the Bible, both to fit me for larger present service and also as important means toward finding God's unfolding plan for my lifework.

"Since thorough training is so valuable in all kinds of Christian service, it is my purpose to secure a college education, if possible."

Dean Luther A. Weigle of the Yale Divinity School, comes at the problem from a helpful angle. He has returned from China where he visited many Christian schools and conferred with Christian leaders generally. The conclusions of these leaders concerning the type of men who should enter the Chinese ministry has something for us. These findings were drawn up at the Kuling conference in the summer of 1935. The primary qualities the Chinese minister needs are: Character first, then mental ability, then sympathy, then information concerning the Bible, the Church and the day in which we live; and last of all, the health and the ability of leadership and an ability to master language in order to actually do the task. The Chinese are keenly aware of their task and they are seeking to find such recruits for their ministry.

The theoretical call must be wedded to the pragmatic fitness and training. One man will feel his call rather than hear it. As Tennyson says:—

If e'er when faith had fall'n asleep
I heard a voice "believe no more,"
And heard an ever breaking shore
That tumbled in the Godless deep;

A warmth within the breast would melt
The freezing reason's colder part,
And like a man in wrath the heart
Stood up and answered, "I have felt."

Preaching proceeds from that personal experience of God who touches me and whom I feel. Our very feelings may yet save us from the folly of our heads.

Pascal writes in his *Thoughts:* "The heart has reasons which the reason does not know. It is the heart that feels God, not the reason."

Here is a man who all his life has wanted to be a physician. He would have made an excellent one. He has read an entire medical library. He has seen a hundred operations. He has set a bone, stitched a scalp when miles from help, and administered ether. "Why are you preaching?" you ask him. Without a single token of misgiving, he smiles back at you, "Medicine is not for me. This is where God wants me." He tells you of a time of struggle and an inner voice.

Here in the correspondence is another: He was offered a college presidency. He wanted it. But it was not for him. "This one thing I do."

And here is another: "I went into a great business house and asked for a Foreign Mission Contribution. I received it and was on the way out, leaving Mr. Hard Boiled with a smile. He called me back. 'How much salary do you get at that church where you preach?'

" 'Three thousand.'

" 'Three thousand! Is that all you get? I'll give you that and more and pay all expenses for you to go into the lumber mills and sell our saws. You came in here and in five minutes are walking out with a good check. And you get it from a hard boiled cuss like me! You're the first fellow to get away with it. How'd you do it? I want you in my business.'

"He didn't even tempt me. It was not for me. Yet," he added, "I'm still wondering how to make ends meet from month to month. But that isn't my calling.

"I'm a called man. God wants me right here and in no other place. When He wants me elsewhere He'll say so."

Here is still another. I give it *in extenso,* with his own interlarded comments just as he sends it. His is a prominent name. You would all know him.

"I was called to preach. I can even give you the day and the hour. I was fourteen years of age. An abnormal experience of turbulent adolescence, perhaps.

"We drove as usual to church on Sunday morning. In our home we had home piety. We had grace at the table, family prayers, and regular church attendance without debate or strife. All the family went. Seeds grow in prepared soil. Calls come to ears and hearts that know what to hear. Calls are heard by souls that have accustomed their spiritual reflexes to respond. That surely is what old Eli told young Samuel. One must not dull his ears by oversleeping the alarm.

"We had just emerged from a revival meeting. It's a very easy thing to say that I was excited. Our emotions were warm and tender. But I for one had not parted with common sense. I had laughed and was still laughing as heartily as any, over the vagaries of the evangelist and had stubbornly resisted him at certain points. I was willing to give my heart to God but I wasn't willing to part company with my mental processes. We do youth a disservice when we think they don't know. They know far more than we give them credit for. That morning father had read at prayers the sixth chapter of Isaiah, 'his train filled the temple.' It was the twenty-third of July and a cold, misty morning. The sexton had chosen it as an appropriate time to light a fire and the flue smoked. The wisp of blue smoke became in poetic imagination the trailing train of Jehovah's robes filling the Temple. Evidently my subconscious mind was stirred. Perhaps a stranger's voice helped to rivet attention. The pastor had exchanged pulpits. The visitor announced his text, 'Arise, he calleth thee.' The church had not yet yielded to the summer slump for the people of that day thought God as essential in summer as winter. We can't expect calls ordinarily where religion is sorely neglected. But there are exceptions to this rule. One deacon and a faithful sister fell asleep shortly after the text was announced. There was no reason why they should not. The sermon could not make them better. They had, like faithful watch dogs, seen the minister through the introduction and scented no heresy. Another deacon was walking up and down a strip of carpet in the rear tending the pastor's baby, while the pastor's wife listened to the sermon. The choir was at the distracting occupation of giggling, gum-chewing, and gossiping. The state of grace of a church choir was written about extensively as long ago as the fourteenth century. In Africa they hire a heathen to beat the tom-tom to call the saints to God's meeting, even now. Nothing about the call interfered with the alert observation of everything that was going on. If a beam from heaven fell that day so also did many reflected beams from the passing scene.

"The sermon was not a remarkable effort. People went to church because it was right and respectable, and in the words of Tennyson's Northern Farmer, 'The preacher said what he thought he ought to ha' said and he comed awa-ay.' But there was one boy there who could not forget the text. All day Sunday and Sunday night and Monday and Monday night and Tuesday and Tuesday night, it was with him. Jesus was by him on the street, and everywhere he could feel Him at his elbow. A gust of wind was the swish of His robe. Tuesday night he went to his room and dreamed. It was the first quiet moment, in turbulence, that he had known. Calvin and all his train believed that when God spoke to the soul he needed a shaft to ride on and the vehicle he chose was always 'The Word.' This call came through a verse of Scripture, read with great conviction by a godly man.

"Dreams have no religious significance. In all seriousness, they are usually the reflection of sex (Freud), or fatigue (Dewey), or waking moments (Watson). Usually they have physical stimuli back of them (James). It is therefore detrimental to the story to intrude the dream, for someone is bound to stop here and say, 'Rank superstition or pure naturalism.' And so it would be if that were all. The only virtue that should be attributed to the dream is that it made his inner conflict clear to his outer mind. It visualized a struggle in the sub-conscious. And while he did not understand it then, it made duty clear. He slept in a little room up under the roof, a room only big enough for a double bed and chair. But the room became precious as his Bethel, for God let down his ladder and angels descended and ascended in blessing. Christ appeared on the cross before him and called him by a name known and used chiefly in the family, and said, 'I have called you to preach and you have refused.'

"In the morning he sought his father. He was greasing the axles of an old wagon. He told him of the dream and of his impressions, adding that he did not want to preach; and even should he so decide, he was so young he might forget, or later change his mind. His father gave no answer to his perplexity, so he told his mother. She saw the realization of her hopes and prayers. That morning the question, 'Is marriage a failure?' dropped completely out of sight from her life, that had been cramped and burdened with life's worries. Like the Suffering Servant of Jehovah in the 53rd of Isaiah, she had 'seen the travail of her soul and was satisfied.' And it could not have been by accident that later in the day, they came into the sitting-room and saw the sewing machine wheeled before the north window where the wild cucumber vine was growing and on the machine an open Bible with these words marked, 'Now, Lord, lettest thou thy servant depart in peace, for mine eyes have seen thy salvation and the glory of thy people, Israel.' And in the light of her angel presence often has his pulpit seemed transfigured. This story he lays as a wreath on Anna Jarvis' grave."

The experience came at fourteen years of age and then was overlaid for years. The joy and assurance of it did not come until at least twenty years later. If the dream had been only a dream I fancy it would have been forgotten. But the dream was only a mile-stone in an experience. The call was not a dream. The call was the wrestling of a soul with the eternal.

None of these men who write me is egotistical. They are testifying to a feeling that they are in the ministry, not only to do good and be a blessing, but because they are chosen men, set apart by the Great Director to play a very definite part in the coming of His Kingdom. The consciousness that they are chosen men has kept them.

There is a gospel to be preached. It is still good news unto salvation. It is still the power of God. God still seeks men and women whom he sets apart for the special service of proclamation. Phillips Brooks was right when he said, "The time must come again . . . when our men shall feel the vitality of the Christian ministry and seek it with heroic consecration."

"There's a fount about to stream,
There's a light about to gleam,
There's a midnight darkness turning into day.
Men of thought, and men of action
Clear the way!"

Shall we be afraid in times like these when we have the real message of hope—the hope of eternal salvation? Have we a god of the Philistines, or the "God of our fathers, living still"? The decision was not ours; it was His: "*I* have chosen you."

CHAPTER IV

THE CONGREGATION MOLDS THE PREACHER

At least one page of this book must be devoted to appreciation of the people whom we serve. The letters of Paul are wet with tears when he speaks of the churches he has founded: Thessalonica, Phillipi, Ephesus. Once does he become severe, when the Galatian region would listen to heresy. When he is writing to Corinth he shows that love can be costly, for after enumerating all the things from which he has suffered: stripes, prisons, shipwreck, robbers, hunger, cold, he adds: "Beside those things, that which cometh daily, the care of all the churches." The churches were Paul's love and Paul's burden. They were to him what the too lusty child is to its frail mother. They made his character and filled his days with supreme joy. They killed him. Their demands took too much from him but how he gloried in it.

Hosea says that a preacher grows to become like his flock. And for the most part this is true, and good. He was an optimist who said the bridegroom does not marry the bride's family. He was more an optimist who thought the pastor could ever be free from his people. Their finances determine the man they invite to lead them. Their intellectual perceptions give color to your thoughts. Their missionary interest determines your zeal. Their friendliness makes you contented to stay. Their appreciation warms your heart while their indifference may dishearten you.

I remember so well the day I stood in the chemistry laboratory with a test tube of mercuric chloride. I dropped in a tiny bit of potassium iodide. The clear poisonous liquid turned blood red. I kept on adding the poison detective a drop at a time. Then came the reaction. The entire substance became clear as crystal. So does one life affect another. So does an aggregate of lives affect another life. So do our congregations change our lives. We have been made by them far more than they have been made by us. Drop by drop they have added a subtle distillation to our thinking until we are changed to our very marrow. Emerson saw this effect of the congregation upon us:

"Nor knowest thou what argument
Thy life to thy neighbor's creed hath lent."

A humanist helped me. I was becoming sour when he found me. "The saints!" I said reproachfully.

He said: "Your congregation want to be your friends. They don't want you to fail. They make excuses for you behind your back when you have a poor day, and you do have poor days. When they speak quickly they are sorry, even though they don't say so. They would say so, if you didn't frighten them. We know little about God. But we can act as if there were one. We can put love into our face and voice in this sad old world. Try it."

He left me with a smile. The effect upon my soul was quick. I said, "Here I am, a Christian minister who knows God, and I go about acting as selfishly and egotistically and sad as if there were no God, while folks with no God go about living as radiantly as if there were one." I resolved then and there to live before every member of my congregation, with

God's help, a minute at a time, as lovingly, as kindly, and as graciously, as if Jesus Christ stood at my elbow. I began to use some muscles in my face that I had not used for a long time.

A Rotarian met me and said, "What's the matter; had your face lifted?" I found some words coming back into my vocabulary. I had called my men, "Old man," when I dared to be familiar and wondered why they did not like it. I now began to say, "Young man," or "Dear fellow," and you would be surprised to see the difference it made. I used to go to my deacons' meetings knowing that they had not done a thing I had asked them to; and they sensed my ill nature over their failure and I came home with a headache—and I deserved it.

I began to consider my situation. I am a proclaimer of ethics; that makes me a judge. I am the voice of eternity; that leaves no room for appeal. I am a salaried man; that puts me at the mercy of the congregation. They are human and sinful; that puts them at my mercy. I too am human; that means that there will be times when I am not at my best. I know the frailties of my people; that would, from the start, naturally incline them to dislike me. It is what the psychologist would call the mother-daughter complex. We preachers have the faults of our very qualities. If we are not careful, people will not love us. If they do not love us, we cannot help them. If we do not love them, we will become scolds. If we love them too much, that is to say, with a spirit of fear or self-protection, or like a grandfather, not caring what they do, we will lose our power over them and cease to be what Ralph Sockman calls us, "men of the mysteries."

So, remembering that the congregation has been given us of God, to love and prepare for His kingdom, let us look at these people as if we never saw them before. Watch out! You are not a country school ma'am stepping into your first school and wondering what big yokel you will have to "lick" first. You are the embodiment of eternal love, with a story to tell, and it will warm their hearts. Look at that congregation and even now after you have been with them five years, more than ninety-five per cent. of them are your friends.

FRIENDS

In that congregation are the friends who have made life richer. They came to us on our first Sunday and said, "Pastor, I didn't vote for you to come. Sometime, perhaps, when the right time comes, I'll tell you why. But you can count on me." And you find you can. They are loyal. That's why they didn't vote for you. They will be by your side when all the world has turned against you. They come to us on the first of each September to welcome us home. There is no effusive greeting. But they quietly say, "Pastor, I want you to meet Mr. Jones. He would like to talk with you about church membership." They are determined that you shall get off to a good start. They spent half of their August vacation to find you that new prospect.

They sat in a committee meeting that you never knew about. Some one had complained about you and was urging your retirement. The vote looked as if it would be, at best, three to three. But your friend said, "Don't you think we'd better pray before the vote is taken. Our pastor is a good man. Perhaps we haven't been patient enough." They knelt and the vote was never taken. You never hear of that meeting until years later.

They saw you only once while you were in the hospital. "I was afraid, pastor, you would have too many visitors." But when you asked for your bill you were told at the window, "The receipted bill is here for you. It's been taken care of." You hobbled wanly to the door, supposing of course that you were being driven home, but instead, you were driven around the lake to a gorgeous country home, where wife awaited you. "What is the meaning of all this, darling?" you asked. And she replied, "You see the Huberts have gone to New York for a month and want us to stay here until they return. The servants will care for us." You are too overcome to ask if it's a business trip or if love planned it.

Friends like that may never tell you so, but they would gladly go forty miles barefoot over frozen ground in your behalf. Every pastor has a surprising number of such. In one church foyer is the beautifully wrought motto, "Please pray for the only one in this church who has no pastor."

No cynicism of the human spirit on blue Monday should blind us to the fact that these friends of ours compose the majority of our congregation. They do for us what a healthy body does for one who toils. They make it possible to carry on.

But there are others in our congregation of whom we must speak. I'm going to be perfectly honest with you for it is part of love to see life whole. It never helped the diagnostician to fool himself by getting but a part of the picture. Sure enough, there he is, that funny little fellow, oh so little, the fault finder. You've got to live with him and save him, too, if you can. He is the son of Shimei who threw stones at

David (II Sam. 16:6). You have thought of him as the fault finding critic. I now think of him as my best friend.

MY BEST FRIEND WAS A GROUCH

He censures you on the slightest pretext and urges the crowd on to laughter at your best efforts. This attitude, I fear, is American. It invades—I do not say pervades—our sanctuaries. Here is a church leader. He believes that he serves God after the strictest sort. If the minister's first sentence magnifies God as on that day this pharisee conceives him, he rubs his phylacteries amiably, and remarks at the close, "Pastor, that was a good sermon. I could have listened for *another hour*. A few more sermons like that and we'll jam the church." But alas! If by way of introduction or illustration the minister is not esteemed so felicitous, he sits moodily, and the next day calls the pastor to complain about something or anything.

There is at least one in nearly every church. Would it be possible for a congregation to recognize him for what he is? I am afraid not. Even he will have his friends and relatives.

How can you live with that curse and be happy about it? Well, if worst comes, you don't have to cultivate him. There is some mental equivalent for switching off the station. Turn the knob on him until you have to meet him again. There are not many like him. Pray for him. Keep your humor.

But almost any person in the church, no matter how difficult, can be shown such attention and such interest, and can be given such careful cultivation, that they will respond to our prayers and our love. The church has very few wilful Judases in it. On every field there will be the exception who must be let alone. But in the main a good rule to follow is to pick out the person who does not seem to care for us and have the fun of turning our greatest liability into one of our quick assets. It can be done. It should be one of our hobbies to see how many grouches we can win over. What a day that always is when some man who has had the reputation of "firing all the ministers" comes to us with a smile and says, "Pastor, do you know, when you first came, I followed afar off. But I've come to feel that you are the best man we've ever had. You can count on me."

The whole theory of social health is grounded in this, that Christianity is imparted by social contact. Ruth was won to the Hebrew faith through Naomi. And Abimelech was lost to the Hebrew faith through a faulty saint. Read Genesis 20. But for one grouch, there will be a hundred others who say of their pastor the equivalent of Stephen Decatur's "My country, right or wrong." After all, preaching does produce the very utmost of understanding and loyalty. Personal loyalty is a choice trait. In its truest form it is blind faith and attachment. It believes in the personality of another so devotedly that it knows whatever one does has back of it a good reason, and that whatever one says is explainable if fully understood. "Though he slay me, yet will I trust him." It is the loyalty of Abraham at Moriah, "God will provide himself a lamb." It is the loyalty of a bride, "for better or worse—I give thee my troth." This is the loyalty that may and should exist between pastor and people. In such an atmosphere hard work becomes easy. A church official went to New York City for an annual meeting on Saturday night. Sunday was to be spent by the delegates in side trips and sightseeing. In the morning he was seen dressing with more than usual care.

"Are you going on the trip?" he was asked.

"Oh no! I always go to church."

His quiet example took more than one hundred men with him.

And again I say you would be perfectly amazed if you could know how many will be loyal to you if given a chance. "This is my pastor." The one who has it brings his friends to the meeting house. "You simply must meet our pastor." It includes the pastor in all the high experiences of life.

But here are some other folks in the congregation, neither friends nor critics. They are the skeptics—they belong to the Thomas family. If you treat these skeptics honestly and respect their personalities they will make a man of you.

THE SKEPTIC

The skeptic is a constant challenge. He challenges your facts: "I have listened to you for nine years and never detected you in a literary blunder until today. You told a story about an Australian boy and attributed it to Stevenson. I think it was a slip of the tongue. But here it is in Charles Reade's *Never Too Late To Mend*. Perhaps you would like to take it." Who will groan angrily at such well meant help? After a few experiences like that you are more careful about facts.

EMBARRASSED!

A friend returned from Italy with one of those lovely and almost priceless ancient illuminated missals from one of the most famous churches in Rome, St. Mary Major. She handed over the precious treasure. "Can you read it?"

It began, "Incip ordo missalis knfuetudenem,"

I read: "Incipit ordo missalis secundum consuetudenim," etc.

I was rather proud of myself to have read seventh century Latin with all its abbreviations. "Can you translate it?"

"The ordo of the missal begins according to the custom of the Roman Curia. The first Sunday of Advent. Station at St. Mary Major. The beginning."

"But what is it all about?"

Now I blushed, for another said, with a bit of malice, "Father Benton of the Franciscan Fathers is in the adjoining room; I'm sure he can tell you about it."

He came in and, taking the scroll in his hands, discoursed learnedly. My banker was facing me with an overdraft. How grateful I have been for that experience. I had been pretty smart. But not as smart as I seemed to be. My skeptical friend discovered me. He had a right to.

The skeptic challenges your philosophy. "My dear pastor, you certainly know that what you said today can't be made to square with John Dewey." You have seen the truth through the eyes of a man honest enough to tell you that you had blundered.

TELESCOPE

Men have been bewildered by the telescope. Copernicus and Galileo and Bruno destroyed a three partitioned universe four hundred years ago. Our problem is no different than the ancient thinker who wrote the 8th Psalm:

"When I consider thy heavens, the work of thy fingers, the moon and the stars, which thou hast ordained; what is man that thou art mindful of him? and the son of man, that thou visitest him?"

Then as now, the crux of the problem was not size. The essential question is the nature of God, man, and reality. Maude Royden with her usual precision put her finger on it, "I suppose," she is reported as saying, "you could put five or six dinosaurs in the Cathedral of St. John the Divine, but if you did, what of it? Could they worship God, or enter into fellowship with Him?"

MICROSCOPE

Some have been bewildered by the microscope. To answer your college youth with a cheap pun and say of evolution, "I've no time to monkey with it," will not win their respect. There is a genetic relation between the empty pews in our churches and a materialistic philosophy to which the man of the street thinks science has forced him. Read to such a man the 139th Psalm. If he will listen to you, get him to pause at the thirteenth verse to tell you what it really says. He may be surprised to discover that it says, God made all things, and man the last of all, but while God doubtless can do anything, His usual method is by the law of normal growth. In some such way your bewildered man may come to see beyond man as an animal, to man as a child of God's handiwork.

MIRROR

Some have been bewildered by the psychological laboratory. Freud and Watson have made it appear that man is simply a set of muscular reactions motivated by the sex impulse with no enucleating soul. This attack for a moment was the most baffling the church had known, until one reflects, that for a psychologist, without an ego, to stand in this strange universe and say, "I see man has no self," would be as self-contradictory as it would be for a blind man to stand before a mirror and say, "I see that I am blind." Any behaviorist who would be believed would better make his own behavior such an outstanding exhibition of morality that men will love his ethics after his philosophy has "gone with the wind."

The skeptic has taught us that the best way to deal with him is to know more than he does. I am grateful to my skeptical friends. They have made me examine and restate my apologetic. They have made me explore the road bed over which human thought travels to see if it is safe. They are not enemies. They are sentries walking the outposts of truth.

THE INDIFFERENT

But the most difficult member of our congregations with which to deal is the one or ones who are neither hot nor cold in their attitudes.

The favorite text of the indifferent man as he yawns in your face is, "Thou never gavest me a kid that I might make merry with my friends."

Dwight L. Moody told this story on himself. "I caused a man to get angry once and he hit me; went at me and knocked me down. It was on the street in Chicago and the fellow was freezing to death; and just before a man freezes he is in a woeful condition. I saw the fellow was freezing and I began to pound him and when he got mad he went for me, and I ran away and left him. And so with church members, I like to pound away at them until they wake up from their indifference."

But why should I be angry or hurt over an indifferent man. The list is long of those who have kept right on preaching. Once upon a time a man came to Dr. Henry G. Weston and said, "Mr. Weston, I don't believe you are the kind of a preacher I like to hear preach." The minister's keen eyes transfixed him as he replied, "My friend, I hope I never will be the kind of a preacher you like to hear." The man went away puzzled and mystified and told his friends about it, and marveled why they laughed.

Sam Jones, the southern pulpit humorist of a past generation, left many kindly intentioned, sun-lit observations about church life behind him. He was called to assist a church that was progressing with difficulty. "What is the matter with us?" they asked. "Well," he replied, after reflection, "about six months ago you asked me down here to pray with you about getting a pastor and I came. We knelt together and you promised the Lord that if he'd send you a preacher, you'd help him draw the gospel wagon. So, God took you at your word. He sent you a preacher and he's a good one. You put him in between the thills of this here one-horse gospel wagon, and then you rascals, instead of getting behind him and praying and pushing, as you said you would, climbed right into the wagon. You're still praying. But I can't find one of you that has done anything to give the wagon a shove forward."

CARNAL SECULARITY

Here is a church where occurred the slow killing of all spiritual graces in a minister of fine mind and interesting life, a gentleman in all his parts. He was called to a church of means, usually known as worldly. Tippling and conviviality were common. The ladies held a successful bridge and raffle annually which netted the church three thousand dollars. The women's missionary society adjourned at three-thirty to the smoking room, after which they reassembled for a session in "solo interpretive dancing as an esthetic expression of religion." Just as a successful traveling man receives a bonus at the end of the year, so the liquor barons of his congregation at the close of the year sent the minister a check to cover a trip to Europe, a new car, a few choice stocks, some expensive furniture. A new stone meeting house was erected. They had costly music. The congregation drifted away. The last printed public utterance of this man was in praise of those days of Queen Anne's reign when rectors went fox-hunting with their squires on Sunday afternoons. He was elected to political office. There are many practices which church people permit themselves of which they do not approve. They would be horrified to find their pastor so employed. The surgeon who operates must do so with aseptic hands. A member of his official board lost his little girl and asked another pastor to officiate.

"Do I have any right to come? Shouldn't you call your own beloved pastor, or at least simply ask me to assist?"

In grim earnestness the member replied: "Please let's not go into that. My wife and I both feel today that we have come to the end of one road and are entering another. I must have for this experience a man who knows God."

The entire story covering the church, the minister, and the official, if true as reported, is unusual, but serves to illustrate the power of a congregation and, even more, the danger inherent in our own nature. Put up your guards when you fight this antagonist, and protect your chin.

THERE'S THE OTHER SIDE OF THE STORY

One remembers that in his own country Jesus "did not many mighty works there because of their unbelief." And one calls also to mind the baffled disciples at the foot of Transfiguration Mountain who were not able to heal the epileptic boy. We shall probably come nearer to the truth if we say that congregation and pastor act and react upon one another in quite decided ways. Neither dares ignore the spiritual impact each is having upon the other. Let the preacher preach as if all depended upon him, but let the congregation remember that it must answer to God for what it does to its minister.

Then, too, the Church should pay its pastor adequately. The government has not made provision for him as a laborer worthy of his hire.

PREACHERS ARE NOT ON THE SOCIAL SECURITY PROGRAM

The pastor must devise a budget on the basis of which he will provide for his future, and he must pay his debts. Some good rules to follow are: Stay on a cash basis. Save a little every year. Talk over the finances with your wife; be partners.

In one church that I served the committee that extended the call asked me to name my own salary. I said, "What would you say to one dollar and all expenses." One of the officials whose perception of monetary values was quicker than his pulse of humor very quickly responded, "Oh no!" He looked up sharply as every one smiled. "We couldn't do that!" Probably to most people we will be a "lazy lot"—gentlemen of starched and elegant leisure, doing our work in indifferent and gorgeous solitude, unless, like William Walsham How, we can break through their resistance by our ministrations of mercy. Of course, to the average man who measures all by the dollar sign, we are in the game for the money. That is why some ministers refuse, if it can be done graciously, to receive personal fees for funerals. If they are received, it can be known that they are administered for the poor and distressed. I suppose the pressure of finances, the desire to ease the burden, if possible, by a larger salary, is responsible for more frequent removals among us than any other reason. But there are more ways to pay a minister than solely with the coin of Cæsar.

WHAT DOES THE LAYMAN WANT?

The safest way to live with folks is to forget one's self and get the other man's viewpoint. The layman has a compartmentalized mind. He is not greatly interested in higher criticism, nor evolution, nor the new theology, nor Russian economic experiments, nor the negro and alien, nor practical efforts to bring in a warless world. He is afraid that these, and each of these, is an effort to rob him of his gospel. He is not a man of the schools at all but a very plain man. He was tempted this week to be dishonest. And his home sanctities have often hung in the balance. He needs you more than you need him.

In a moment of anger he was profane, and it still troubles him. The banker refused to renew his loan, and he wonders if he can discount his bills this week. He is not thinking of you any more than the very sick patient is thinking of the nurse. You are not there to be babied. You are there to help him. He needs sympathy, understanding and encouragement. He wants a faith that will make him faithful and get him through the week. He knew his mother had religion. He would have it too. He hopes you will help him to get a real faith, and not trot out any more of those fool notions that you talked about last week. You may count on his listening for the first three minutes. He will listen longer if you are helpful enough. He does not care about your sermon being a masterpiece either, for he will hear an address just as bad or worse at Kiwanis next Wednesday. If you choose an old hymn that he knew when a boy, you will predispose him in your favor. If you are a bit nervous he will like that too. He will remember the last speech he gave at the club and he will tell his wife at dinner that you are not as high and mighty as he thought you were at first. Particularly will he say so, if your voice broke when you prayed for the shut-ins. His mother sat in a wheel-chair the last three years of her life. As a boy he knew direst poverty. He worked hard and practiced thrift for every cent he possesses. No one ever thinks of thanking him when he gets to work on time and is tired when the day's work is done. He does not see why you should have preferential treatment.

HE WANTS TO BE TREATED LIKE AN ADULT

He does not care for Shirley Temple films. And he does not want you to play the juvenile.

A missionary's widow with her very little son returned from Persia for a furlough. After a few years the two returned to Persia, but meanwhile the boy had learned to love the United States and to weigh its advantages. At the end of the long journey they paused and looked down from a hill top upon the brown mud huts of the village and the dreary location of the mission compound. Presently the child said, "Mother, this isn't half as nice as in America." The first realization swept his soul like a tempest as he stood there disconsolately, appreciating all they had left. His wise mother waited a moment and then she said: "I know it, laddie; that's why we've come."

The power of the church over its minister is exercised daily across our land, chiefly for good. Our people, even those who act as a drag upon our soaring spirits, in the long run would condemn us for lowering the sanctions under which we operate. They are probably as unaware of their power to hurt us as a typhoid carrier is that he spreads the pestilence. They don't want to do it. And most of them do not. The vast majority are, as Jesus said, "salt," and "light," and "leaven in the meal."

In the great day there will be many a captain who now thinks himself sorely abused who will call his ranks to attention before the reviewing stand and make report to our Great Captain: "Of them whom thou gavest me I have lost none," and toward that hour of joy he now looks, in moments of truest insight, with awe and deathless longing.

CHAPTER V

JESUS SAID IT THUS

Jesus honored preaching. In His thought and practice it outreached healing and general philanthropy. "He went through all their cities preaching the gospel of the Kingdom." "I must preach, for therefore am I sent." "The common people heard him gladly."

The Gospel of Matthew is builded around five sermons of Jesus. The first of these is often called "The Sermon on the Mount," but probably Jesus would have said it was His sermon on "the Kingdom." The second, Matthew 10, is on "Apostleship." The third, Matthew 13, with the parable of the four kinds of soil for its introduction, is a sermon on "How to Enter the Kingdom." The fourth, Matthew 16, is a brief address upon "Man and His Need of the Kingdom." The fifth and last is, in reality, a combination of two sermons, as Matthew makes plain. In the first of these, Matthew 21:23 to Matthew 23:39, He speaks of Himself as the "Founder of the Kingdom," and in the second, on "The Triumph of the Kingdom" (Matthew 24: and 25). Jesus was a prodigious worker and his sermons show it.

A casual examination of the Gospel according to Matthew shows that Jesus quoted eleven books of the Old Testament thirty-two times, and showed perfect familiarity with its substance and interpretation. For purposes of reference these texts are here given.

Genesis 1:27; 2:24; Exodus 3:6; 20:12-16; 21:17-24; Leviticus 13:49; 14:2; 19:12-18; 20:9; 24:20; Numbers 30:2; Deuteronomy 5:12-20; 6:5; 19:21; 23:21; 24:1-4; 25:5; Psalm 8:2; 22:1; 78:2 (?); 110: 1; 118:22; Isaiah 42:1 (?); 61:7; 62:11 (?); Jeremiah 7:11; Daniel 9:27; 11:31; 12:11; Hosea 6:6; Zechariah 9:9 (?); 13:7.

THE SERMON ON THE MOUNT HAD CERTITUDE

Jesus' preaching had in it certitude. "He taught them as one having authority." It is a part of the pity of the present moment that we are not even sure of this. We seem unable to say with the men of the first century, "We know that thou art a teacher come from God," nor with the men of the fourth century, "Thou art the King of Glory, Oh Christ," nor even with Emerson, "He is the highest revelation mankind has yet received of God." We vacillate about His person, His message, His work, His destiny.

A physician was called in on a case. "The honest truth is I do not know what ails your child. I doubt if any one knows." The hard-headed, soft-hearted father, just home from the day's grind at the mills, without a moment's hesitation said, "Well, doc, I admire your honesty, but you're fired. I'm goin' to get a man to help my sick little girl that knows, or at least thinks he does."

The Lord Bishop of London and Betterton, the famous English actor, were friends. "Why," asked the Lord Bishop, "do the crowds leave me to go to your house of make-believe?" Betterton's answer was, "You in the pulpit *tell* a story. We on the stage *show* the facts."

THE SERMON ON THE MOUNT WAS ELOQUENT

Jesus was incomparably eloquent. Eloquence is undesirable when it attracts men only to a human personality. Oratory of itself is like a mist or fog. Its value is in the residue it precipitates.

Perhaps Talmage and Moody may be compared. Talmage was by far the greatest pulpit orator of his day whether judged by crowds or by the millions who read his addresses. His so-called pulpit power exceeded any of his contemporaries, Moody, Brooks, or Beecher. Yet upon his death his church disappeared like a crowd from a movie. Moody was far less an orator, but his work lives on now after a hundred years. He built Northfield and Mount Hermon, the Moody Church, the Moody Colportage Association, and best of all lives on in the lives of John R. Mott, Sherwood Eddy, Robert E. Speer, Henry Drummond, and many others.

JESUS' GESTURES

How many times it says, "And he looking round about upon them," or "he lifted his eyes." The eye is as mighty in its power of gesture as the hand. Can any one who ever heard Woodrow Wilson speak have forgotten those eyes! They missed nothing. They created sympathy and understanding. Even his keenest enemies noticed this, and it filled them with fear of his power. Why should we leave the power of expressive gesture through the eye to an unlettered colored singer, an Eddie Cantor, or a courtesan.

JESUS FELT DEEPLY

Fear of feeling is a sophistication. It is a late growth upon the rotten limb of a too old society. Youth and health never fear feeling. And eloquence is compact of correct feeling. Every scene that youth most truly loves: engagements, weddings, birthdays, games, parties, sports, movies, war, spectacles, are all compact with feelings. So long as the moon is in the sky, so long as the lights burn low, so long as the flag waves, so long as invitations are sent, so long will feeling endure. Our only care should be to see that eloquence expresses upon as noble a plane as the greatest in music and art, the higher emotions of the soul. John Bunyan says of his own preaching: "I preached what I felt—what I smartingly did feel, even that under which my poor soul did groan and stumble . . . After two years the Lord came in upon my soul in comfort through Christ . . . I showed them this also."

JESUS WAS AN ANALYST

We are in a temporary mood that belittles the skeleton of the sermon. We are told to keep it out of sight. Perhaps the old pulpiteers overdid it, wandering on endlessly to their seventeenthlies. Numerous stories are told all to the same point that the preacher did not know when to stop. But the simple fact is that no sermon will be either clear or rememberable that does not have a carefully prepared outline.

Let us study for organizational outline:

THE SERMON ON THE MOUNT

MATTHEW 5-7

Introduction

The paradoxical Beatitudes, like all introductions were given to arouse attention. 5:1-12.

I. The Purpose of the Christian Movement is to Establish the Kingdom. 5:13-16.
  1. It is to save men and society.
    (1. As salt saves.
    (2. As light saves.

II. The Relation of the Kingdom to Judaism. 5:17-20.
  1. Is not that of destruction but fulfillment.
    (1. Consider the Mosaic Law:
      a. the law of murder. 5:21-26.
      b. the law of adultery. 5:27-32.
      c. the law of oaths. 5:33-37.
    (2. Consider Love. 5:38-48.

III. The Relation of the Kingdom to Prophetic Ethics is
  1. Again, fulfillment, 6:1a.
    (1. Consider:
      a. almsgiving. 6:2-4.
      b. prayer. 6:5-15.
      c. fasting. 6:16-18.
      d. mammon. 6:19-34.
      e. censoriousness. 7:1-6.

IV. How Shall Men Obtain the Kingdom?
  1. Ask for it of God. 7:7-11. This is faith.
  2. Strive for it. 7:12-14. This is works.

V. In Conclusion. Act on what you know.
  1. Don't argue. 7:15-23.
  2. Do it now; obey my teaching; accept my Messiahship; build on the Rock. 7:24-27.

THE SERMON ON THE MOUNT WAS ETHICAL

Jesus' preaching was ethical. Probably this is what a student of Jesus' teaching most quickly sees. The heart of His system is, of course, love, judged in the light of a golden rule. "Would you say such conduct was loving if one acted so toward you?" He asks. But it takes scant discernment to see that to be able to live on such a plane of love demands a moral miracle. And so Jesus' preaching of ethics is always undergirded with the moral power He imparts to live ethically. Preaching on moral issues such as war, economics, greed, race hatred, sex transgression, liquor, and such like, is necessary. But it will be unavailing of itself, alone; it must be accompanied by the Spirit of God and personal surrender.

JESUS' PREACHING WAS BACKED BY HIS LIFE

"I'd rather see a sermon than to hear one any day,
I'd rather one should walk with me than merely tell the way.
The eye's a better pupil and more willing than the ear,
Fine counsel is confusing, but example's always clear,
And best of all the preachers are the men who live their creeds,
For to see good put in action is what everybody needs." *

JESUS PREACHING EXPECTED RESULTS

In every instance of which we have record Jesus closed His sermon expecting a definite and immediate response. This has always been the test of the speaker. When the old lion, Demosthenes, had finished his "Oration on the Crown," he

* The quotation is from Edgar A. Guest's poem, "Sermons We See," found in his copyrighted book of verse, *The Light of Faith,* and used by permission of the author and the publishers, Reilly and Lee Co., Chicago, Ill.

demanded an immediate vote that sent his opponent, Æschines, into exile. In the Roman Senate, the elder Cato finished speaking, and they reached for their swords and echoed, "Carthago delendo est." It is a sound psychological perception which affirms that a speech of persuasion must end in some kind of action. The minister must provide some outlet for the energies of the soul. Does he wish decision to enter the Christian life, then the immediate opportunity must be provided in some fashion, by card, or hand, or rising, or coming down the aisle, or by an opportunity for conferences. Aimless exhortation gets one nowhere except further backward. Try to build each of those six elements of Jesus' sermon into your next week's sermon. Do it with confidence and with a prayer that He will show you how. Then see what is its effect?

CHAPTER VI

EFFECTIVENESS IN PRESENTING THE CHRISTIAN MESSAGE

The preacher will work carefully to make the manuscript of his sermon a perfect piece of literary and grammatical construction. But when once he has done his best, he will remember that the spoken utterance has about it a fine sense of abandon.

The old Welshman listened carefully to a sermon that was rather too well done and drily said, "Sir, but waren't it fine? But it were all to be consumed on the premises. It waren't to be carried away."

Occasionally, a Saturday of preparation will come like this: we are interrupted by two funerals, a three hundred mile drive, home at three o'clock Sunday morning. We *must* preach in the morning and evening, teach a men's class, and conduct another funeral.

There is no "if," "and," or "but" about it. Under any ordinary rules of the game we would fail. But that Sunday we do our best work. The superficial man will emerge from such an experience believing that he has been too anxious and singleminded about his preparation. He forgets three things. That God comes to the aid of the man who needs and asks; that the best befalls only a mind richly stored; and that there are areas of the brain we use only in an emergency. It would almost seem as if the hard labor of such a day set all the brain cells vibrating so that they do work otherwise impossible, just as the vibrations of a cello "make" the orchestra, or as a deaf man hears best in the din of a train. The wise man will not be deceived by such an experience. Preaching demands labor.

Austin Phelps defines the sermon as "an oral address, delivered before a popular audience, on a religious subject, based upon the Scriptures, elaborately treated, and whose purpose is the persuasion of the hearer."

How shall we make such a sermon a success? Here are eight rules that have proven effective.

Rule One: The sermon will be scriptural.

The Bible is a body of literature, in which is crystallized the best religious consciousness of mankind, sustained through vast periods of history, and energized, guided and controlled by the Spirit of God. God is partially revealed in the history and literature of the Old Testament, but finds full orbed revelation in Jesus Christ. The sermon reveals God and interprets Holy Scripture. The minister seeks, in the Bible and in his own experience of Christ, a concept of a saving God and this he imparts to his hearers. "What the eternal says I stammering say again."

The artist is the consciousness of the whole world in relation to art. The minister is the consciousness of the universe regarding religion, voiced to a congregation. We are not prophets of the obvious.

Some one enquires, "Is a text indispensable for a sermon?" In raising the question they remark that for twelve hundred years the sermon was delivered without a text and that for the next seven hundred years the text was closely adhered to. Both the Old and New Testament seem to indicate that post-reformation usage is a return to an earlier norm.

The return to religion under Josiah recorded in II Kings 22 and 23 was brought about through a perusal of Scripture. The reforms under Nehemiah and Ezra were accomplished in the same manner (cp. Nehemiah 8:1-8). Jesus' sermon in Nazareth was the exposition of Isaiah 61:1. Peter's sermon at Pentacost was preached from Joel 2:28. Philip preached to the Eunuch from Isaiah 53:7 and Stephen in his famous defence, gave a running commentary on all Old Testament history, dwelling particularly upon Deuteronomy and Amos and Isaiah. Our preaching must be the authentic word from God, growing out of insight and revelation.

In Greek architecture the ornamentation is an essential part of the building itself. To remove it one must demolish the structure. In Roman architecture, the building is constructed and the ornamentation is added afterward as a sort of afterthought which is not essential.

The idea is the same as that of a bride's veil at a wedding, desirable and beautiful for the more formal occasions but non-essential. It is after this Latin idea that many sermon builders have written their sermon, and then looked about for a text with which to adorn it. We cannot recommend it, any more than we can recommend dead-reckoning to a sea captain. There is much about the stars we do not know, but the mariner still feels they are good to steer by.

We acknowledge that textual preaching runs the danger of becoming senile, repetitious and wooden. We plead for a "word" that is "made flesh" and that "dwells among us."

At the age of thirty-three Dr. MacLaren was called to occupy one of the most influential pulpits in Great Britain. At that time he explained his ambition as a preacher, which was to concentrate his whole strength upon the proclamation of the gospel from the pulpit. "Many people in the congregation," he wrote, "wish simple Bible preaching. Now I feel that I have a great deal more sympathy with this class of people than I had. I have learned, I shall never unlearn, lessons that after all our sole power lies in the true, simple, sincere setting forth of the living Christ, and I abjure forevermore all the rubbish of intellectual preaching. I would rather serve out slops for the people to live upon than lumps of stone cut into the forms of loaves."

Rule Two: The sermon must be brief; keep it to the point.

One has only thirty minutes in which to preach. Run beyond the twelve o'clock hour just once and see what happens. If for any reason it is eleven thirty-five when you start, still you must close at twelve. Say what you have to say briefly. Come to the point. The whole modern tendency is in your favor.

George Washington signed his letters by hand, "I have the honor to remain, Sir, your most respectful and obedient servant," but today the signature of all of us is, "Yours truly," and we even rubber stamp it "Dictated but not read."

Without brevity we will find ourselves members of the guild of Postlude Artists who "play them out." If the congregation are growing restless, we are the umpire, and must call the game on account of darkness. Study the technique of the prize fighter: he packs a mighty wallop in a short blow. Consider Edward Everett's three-hour oration. Then consider that it was Lincoln's Gettysburg address that every one remembers.

Lamb tells us of being captured by Coleridge in the Strand, who seized hold of a coat button, and began to drill Lamb's ear. After a half hour, Lamb cut off the button and went his way. That night when Lamb returned Coleridge was still there discoursing away. No one but Lamb could so perfectly hit off the bore.

Rule Three: The sermon will be simple; clarify it.

The wisest speakers, while they will dwell on great themes, are always rudimentary, assuming that there are those in the audience who know nothing of the subject and using great care to make plain the meaning of any necessary technical phrases.

Clarity is difficult. We carry a watch and drive a car. But who could put either one together. We take the difficult too much as a matter of course. My friend the florist and my friend the musician were talking. One mentioned the "Scherzo in C Sharp Minor by Chopin," and the other "Aphis Major in Rosacea Spiræa Americanis," and both thought themselves talking of the same thing, and they had the grandest time. The constant temptation is to substitute eloquence for clear speech.

Simplicity includes positive affirmation. A successful French physician who was asked the secret of his healing art, said, "Il affirme." Of Jesus it is said, "In him was yea." Our most effective strategy will always be, not in attacking error but in binding up truth. To show where one diverges in view will only awaken antagonism. Goethe said, "Keep your doubts to yourself. I have enough of my own. Tell me your convictions."

Humility is a virtue. "Humility, that low sweet root, from which all heavenly virtues shoot." But humility as a personal trait must never affect our faith in our message. Cowper seems to have had the minister in mind when he wrote:

"With hesitation admirably slow
He humbly hopes—presumes—it may be so.
He would not in a preemptory tone,
Assert the nose upon his face his own."

Simplicity sometimes requires the use of vocal force. But one must constantly remember not to use the hammer for long. The most deadly and mind-breaking monotony one's ears ever hear is that of the air drill. One must sustain his tone to be heard, and interest will be secured by variety of intonation.

While browsing in the public library one day we found a book of sermons by an English clergyman, published a half century ago. Letting the pages run through one's fingers and picking at random here is a fair sample: "The incomprehensibility of the apparatus developed in the machinery of the universe may be considered a supereminent manifestation of stupendous majesties whether a man stands on the platform of his own mind and ponders scrutinizingly on its undecipherable characters or whether he looks abroad over the magnificent equipments and regalities of nature surveying its amplitudes in all their profundities." What was he saying? Probably the same as the psalmist in Psalm 8:3, "When I consider the heavens, the work of thy fingers, the moon and the stars thou hast ordained, what is man that thou art mindful of him?" But one cannot be sure. Such so-called preaching is monstrous trifling with the gospel in what Dr. David Burrell of sainted memory with fine scorn would call "sesquipedalian phrases."

On the Tea Wharf in Boston they still tell among the candle drippings in an upper room, of Father Taylor, famous preacher to sailors, who became involved in a long sentence and ended, "I have no idea where I started, nor where I am going, but I'm on my way to the Kingdom of God, and there I would take you."

Rule Four: The sermon will be emotional; feel it.

The preacher's primary emotion will of course be love. Jesus said, "Love the Lord thy God . . . and thy neighbor." No power we possess so greatly influences life, as letting people see that we genuinely like them.

The effective sermon is never a scolding sermon. We must cultivate in our own nature radiance, joy, and love. Watch the muscles of your own face. Intense thought will draw the lines down, if one is not careful. Consciously relax. Make it a habit. Meet difficulties with the relaxed mind. Babies can take bumps that would kill an adult because their muscles are relaxed. The muscles and the mind are bound up together. Love folks.

One must also feel the surging emotions of the whole scene. You are compassed about by a great cloud of witnesses. Your whole performance is before a cosmic back-drop that takes in God, angels, saints and men. Your own nature has felt the tug of mighty forces. You have known the contending armies that your audience feel and fear. Twice, once in the Old Testament (Dan. 10:13), and once in the New (Jude 13), the author senses the personal struggle in terms of a larger stage. This theme Paul continually comes back to: "We wrestle not against flesh and blood, but against principalities, against powers, against the rulers of the darkness of this world."

Billy Bray, the eccentric Cornish miner, who during the week worked below ground in the mines, but on Sundays exhorted and built chapels was reproved on one occasion for working overtime, in pious vociferation. He retorted on this wise: "Why, boys! If you's head me h'up in a barrel, Oid shout 'Glory 'Allelujah', through the bunghole!"

The dangers of enthusiasm are obvious but cold-blooded intellectualism has even more grave dangers. Study the following passage from the farewell address of Elihu Root on quitting public office.

> "Mr. Chairman, there is a plain old house in the hills of Oneida, overlooking the valley of the Mohawk, where truth and honor dwelt in my youth. When I go back, as I am about to go, to spend my declining years, I mean to go with the feeling that I can say I have not failed to speak and act in accordance with the lessons that I learned there from the God of my fathers. God grant this opportunity for service to our country and our state may not be neglected by any of the men for whom I feel so deep friendship in this convention."

As Mr. Root concluded, his voice broke with emotion and there were tears in many eyes. It is impossible, even if it were necessary, to reach such an altitude of emotion fifty-two times a year, but the appeal of the pulpit would be more effective, when tremendous moral earnestness is in evidence. Mr. Root in his great career did not simply play upon emotions; he transformed their emotions into motions—he changed votes.

Rule Five: The sermon must be well illustrated; picture it.

Dr. Thomas Guthrie who in his day spoke to thousands of the plain people counseled his brethren to hard labor. "In preaching one must prove to the reason, arouse the fancy by painting pictures for the heart, and persuade the will. Like my Master I illustrate my sermons, for 'without a parable spake he not unto them.'"

Do not let people date you by your anecdotage. Use stories but use them sparingly. Do not acquire a name as a story teller. If they are to be told let them be to the point, never irreverent, and never vulgar. The better the illustration the less possible will it be to use it more than once, as it will the more likely be remembered.

Jesus used stories effectively. Recall the story of the prodigal son. Seek your illustrations in papers and books, in nature, in the Bible, in home and in business. Never apologize for the citation of a personal experience if it is a good illustration. Religion is a personal experience. Preaching when it leaves the area of personal experience is arid.

Quote poetry. Some possessing a photographic memory learn easily. Such persons will tend to overdo the matter of quotation. Some, with almost no verbal memory, rarely use poetry. There should be some way to even things up. Make yourself learn some apt quotation and use it.

Clip and preserve in a file your illustrations. A good illustration used appropriately is worth half a sermon. Perhaps it will be remembered long after the sermon is forgotten.

Occasionally start the sermon with a story. Dr. J. B. Jeter and Dr. John A. Broadus were once scheduled to speak at a great religious convention. Dr. Jeter made the first address upon the sacrifice of Christ, taking as his text John 3:16. He delivered a mighty discourse but it called forth little interest and no enthusiasm. Dr. Broadus then began his address by telling of a little boat lightly moored at the side of a river. A dog jumped on, and while gamboling about, the boat became loosened and floated out into the stream. Soon it moved faster and faster—it was approaching the falls—and the frightened dog went from side to side, yelping in terror. Along flew the boat, passing rocks, trees and points of land, rapidly nearing the tremendous falls, the dog howling piteously. All at once, Dr. Broadus, noticing the strained attention of the audience, stopped short, and then said, "My good friends, are you not ashamed to be so worked up over the fate of a dog which could, in the last event, probably swim to shore, and yet sit here with indifferent looks and feelings while Dr. Jeter has been portraying to you the tragedy of the world."

Illustrations are to the sermon what the love interest is to a modern romance. They are to the sermon what human interest is to a news reporter. Have you noticed that in every still picture the interest centers in a living object. Illustration likewise affords the necessary focus of interest.

Illustrations have been frowned upon. The man who used them has been thought shallow. But this is only because the illustration was not carefully chosen. One may cheat in their use. Death-bed stories and all pathos must be used sparingly and with discretion, if at all. But one may no more preach without illustrations than one may have a wedding without the bride; or drive his car without gasoline.

Rule Six: Gestures have a proper place in every sermon; use them carefully.

Imagine Jesus speaking to the rich young ruler. "Go sell all that thou hast." Would He say that in a tone of stern command, mild enquiry, entreating love or retarded vexation? How do you think His eyes looked? His hands? How did His voice vibrate? How would He speak to Nicodemus? Or to the woman by the well?—"Go, call thy husband." Or to Judas?—"What thou doest do quickly." Some time try to tell your audience simply by tone and inflection precisely what Jesus said by a gesture. The movie artists, with a lifted eyebrow, a shrug, a silence, a hand toying with a flower, express themselves often far more eloquently than by word.

The mirror may be an advantage if it does not make of us self-conscious actors, straining after effect. The best gestures are always unconscious.

One famous orator paused and said, "To what shall I liken it?" He looked about the stage bewilderedly, seeking the appropriate object of the moment to adorn his tale. He found it in a glass of water. He dipped his finger in it ever so lightly, then held it aloft and waited for a drop of water to fall. Its effectiveness lay in its apparent spontaneity. But it had all been rehearsed. It was superb until one heard it the second time.

Gestures can be overdone. An exhorter preaching on, "and the door was shut," threw himself against the pulpit door shouting, "Noah, let us in." The door flew open and another pharisee received his reward in a bad fall.

Whitfield on the other hand was so gracious in gesture that people forgot his squinting vision. One would hardly say "Come to Jesus," with a clenched fist.

The sources of natural gesture lie within one's own spirit. It is for this reason that one's life must be pure, and filled with communion with God. Otherwise the Mount Vesuvius of one's nature may overflow at any moment. (Matt. 15:16-20.)

Faulty gestures may be cute in a young theologue, as stuttering may be cute in a debutante, but both become impossible, wearisome and disgusting in age.

Yesterday I attended a great down-town religious gathering.

A metropolitan minister spoke. He was well dressed. He had a carefully prepared address. Had it been given over the radio it would have been a capital performance. He was nervous. His mannerisms destroyed the comfort and the attention of an audience unused to his eccentricities. I made a note of what he did. He clutched his finger, clawed the air, bulged his lower lip, wiped the corners of his mouth and consulted his notes. He clenched his fist, scratched his nose, felt of his cheek and ear and consulted his notes. He grabbed and wrinkled his coat lapel and consulted his notes. He stuffed his hands into his pockets, took them out again, crossed his arms, snorted and cleared his throat, threw out his chest in defiance, and noisily consulted his notes. He bent forward at a right angle, covered his mouth, teetered a little, removed his glasses and cleaned them and consulted his notes. He wiped his nose with his finger with an intake of breath, thought better of it, secured a handkerchief, after fumbling, and used it, dabbing his nose, city style; was disappointed with the performance and went back at it again much more noisily, vigorously and thoroughly. Looked satisfied and put the handkerchief away. He now thought for a moment. What part of his anatomy should be open to inspection next? He scratched his head, smoothed his hair, stood on one leg with knee drawn up and in this position crossed his arms behind his back. When two way traffic was resumed he consulted his notes. He lowered his voice to an impressive whisper, but the whisper came on the last and most important word and none got the point beyond the first five rows. He leaned heavily on the pulpit, squinted, cleared his throat loudly and swung heavily with rhythm, accenting each word.

He made a great speech, the paper said. It would have

been much better if all had listened. I was prevented from hearing by a deterrent personality. He suffered from static. His address was a physical mistake. Seemingly he was unaware that gestures are a part of the sermon. And his best friend will not tell him!

Rule Seven: A sermon should be delivered extemporaneously; deliver it without notes.

I am conscious that this runs counter to much clerical opinion.

James G. Blaine once told a group of preachers in Maine, "Gentlemen, your manuscript is a non-conductor." If I were the professor of homiletics in a seminary, I would give a passing mark to no student who did not give promise of being an extemporaneous speaker. By extemporaneous speaking is not meant pure improvisation. This is always dangerous. The extemporaneous speaker having thought and read deeply, written carefully, outlined completely, trusts his verbiage to the moment. Such men, when attorneys at law, are always most successful with the jury.

There will be certain ministers who will think they find the extemporaneous method disadvantageous, for want of natural aptitude, or because of the variableness of their own moods. Of course, it will be difficult and, at first, well nigh impossible.

It will be necessary to train the memory. But this can be done by various devices. You wish to remember arguments or incidents. List them geographically if you can and travel in a sequential order, from New York, to London, to Bombay, to Osaka, to Seattle. That is an orderly arrangement from west to east. New York, Osaka, Seattle, London, Bombay, would not do. Sometimes one can list them in accordance with the orderly sequences of the body, the head representing the mind, the chest representing the affections, the legs representing the will to serve. Take for yourself the seven deadly sins and arrange them in a mnemonic order that your mind will accept. Do the same with the seven last words of Christ. Visualize the scene. Prostrate on the ground while the nails were driven, "Father, forgive." Raised between the thieves, "Today, with me." The first downward look, "Mother, thy son." Now for the first time a moment to think, "Eloi." After the agony of soul passed, only then conscious of a body, "I thirst." It is near the end now. "Tetelestai—it is finished." And last, "Into thy hands."

Try the same with the twelve disciples. And the ten commands. And the seven churches of Asia.

A thing to be remembered can always be pictured to the mind. Alliteration may help. "Pardon, peace and power." The acrostic has its uses. I know that the acrostic method is the lazy man's method of building a sermon. I do not advocate it. But I also know that sometimes when the sermon is prepared it can be rearranged into an acrostic order for purposes of memory. Here is the word Faith. It begins in

1. F—Forgiveness of sin.
2. A—Attachment to a person.
3. I—Interest in a cause.
4. T—Triumph over obstacles.
5. H—Heaven at last.

Cheap, do you say? Rememberable, I answer. A sermon must be remembered. If you cannot remember it your people will not. Any basket is good which will carry your groceries.

Any memory device is permissible which helps you to fulfill your errand.

A certain diffuseness of style is not to be frowned upon. It is to the mind what roughage is to the alimentary tract. The wave of attention in the average mind does not exceed three minutes in length. An address that is too packed in style will leave its hearers gasping for breath, drowned in words, the meaning of which never reached the listeners. There are always those who say they cannot speak extemporaneously because of nerves.

All the greatest preachers have always had a certain amount of stage fright. Spurgeon had it and so did Beecher and Brooks. All the great athletes have it, too, before they contend in games, and Sara Bernhardt had it until she thought she would die. But every one of these came to know that without it they never did their best. If they were alert, eager, apprehensive, aware of the possibilities of failure, aware of what the crowd needed, they knew they would do well. On days when it was lacking it seemed a foreboding of failure. It became the mark of their power, for which they watched eagerly. A great prima donna once envied a speaker his poise. He said to her: "My dear, I was terribly nervous."

"But you didn't show it."

"No and neither do you. You seem so calm. It is your nerves and temperament that have made you the queen of song."

Sometimes nerves affect the memory. That is because in one's preparation one had not consciously visualized the audience as a component part of the speech. Some speakers will do better to sit in the audience quietly until their turn comes, but these are in the minority. The greater number should face the audience and become aware of the sea of faces and adjust the mind to it. The actor is protected from this by footlights, but there is no such protective screen of light from the preacher. Every speaker, some time or another, will face a complete blank, when the address leaves him. The only thing to do in such a moment, is not to fumble or grope, in hope of finding the word or thought. One must quickly, unconcernedly, turn to something quite different and talk of it. Usually in a few minutes the mind will bring back the straggling truant. No one will know the battle and victory but yourself. A very prominent minister of the Mississippi valley confessed that this occurred to him. "I could not think of my text, my subject, my divisions, my illustrations." He had behind him years of experience and power. "My eye caught my ring. I held up my left hand and said, 'Do you see that ring? I want to tell you about it.'" He told of how it came into his possession. He told of the heart throbs back of it. At the close of the recital his mind, that had played him false, was suing for forgiveness and had brought back all the stolen plunder and laid it at his feet. He preached the sermon as if nothing had happened.

Dr. Wm. M. Lawrence of Chicago arose to announce the text just as a band blared by. He did not recover himself quickly, and so quietly dismissed the congregation with the benediction. The congregation did not hold it against him. They loved him the more, because "he was in all points like as they."

Rule Eight: Blessed is the preacher who is expecting a decision. Apply your sermon and win your verdict; be specific.

Within any congregation he will find three fundamental elements of resistance. The first is physical: "We are really tired. We are all indifferent. We are all inert. You cannot interest us." The second is personal: "The man has a good line. He's interesting some. But there's nothing in it for me." The third is pugilistic: "Come, come now. I've been very patient with you. I defy you to prove your case."

In a Christian congregation this may be followed by the attitude of penitence and procrastination. "Almost thou persuadest me to be a Christian. I believe what he says. I'd like to. But not today."

It is at this point that the minister's power will be most tested. He is now like the runner in the four hundred yard race. Has he endurance and stamina to stand up to the very end and cross the tape to victory?

Dr. Shailer Mathews used to tell us we were not in the pulpit to conduct a Cook's tour, but to create a Crusader's interest.

The art of finishing is the great art, and the old French preachers had for a favorite maxim that a "fire in the exordium is a fire in straw." The main thing was how a man came out at the end. Did he bring his truth through? A good critic of sermons said that with most preachers there was a point where, no matter how well they had done up to that point, they began to break down, to lose grip of their matter and confidence in it. And when he saw a preacher reaching that point, but passing through it and seizing his message with a new grip from there on to the end, then he knew that man had felt celestial fire.

The final test of every sermon is this: Did I win the man I went after for Christ? The sermon is a vehicle to that one end. Lengthen, alter, shorten, improvise, change—but get your verdict!

CHAPTER VII

HAVE THY TOOLS READY; GOD WILL FIND THE WORK

AFTER the sermon, no minister has a right to associate with any but those he loves. The buoyancy one feels after a "great effort" may lead him to do or say foolish things. One is more likely to be off his guard. Recall that Philip after the conversion of the Eunuch was "caught away, and was found in Azotus." The story of the old prophet in I Kings 13:11 is worth reading. "Thou shalt eat no bread nor drink water there." If some one could only take us when the sermon is done and shelter us. God help us, when the sermon is done! It may help us to remember that after the flask of nard was broken the aroma filled the room. Mary's vase was not sorry. For the Master saw and was satisfied.

One's preparation for the following Sunday begins on Sunday night when one switches off the light and forgets his errors.

"Did any one tell you it was a good sermon?" The minister must quickly get past that stile. Some of your best sermons you will never hear from until long afterward. Spurgeon was once told by the flatterer at the foot of the pulpit stairs, "Oh, Mr. Spurgeon, that was a great sermon," and he saved his humility and showed his good sense by remarking, "Yes, the devil told me that the moment I had finished."

An occasional sermon must be so much to the point that

none will like it. There is a proverb which says, "a few think today what many will utter tomorrow."

Lowell tells us that we do not know the moment when fate takes our measure and says to us that it finds us ready. Kingsley has almost an identical word, "Have thy tools ready; God will find the work." Not Sunday only, but each of the preacher's days should be filled with toil. We are not working by the piece, but by the job. Our work is done when our day is done, and the fever of life is past, and the evening shadows lengthen. Start the day with God. Near my Bible and my reading glasses where I can reach them easily when I awake, I keep à Kempis and Augustine and Phelp's *Still Hour,* and Matheson's *Times of Retirement,* and Havergal's *Kept for the Master's Use,* and Speer's *Remember Jesus Christ,* and a dozen more. I try to be a Christian man. The church is my twenty-four-hour, seven-day, fifty-two-week, every-year business, and I love it.

THE SILENT WITNESS TO OUR PREACHING

Much of our real preaching will be indirect preaching. It will be the silent witness of our entire life, from the way we wear our clothes and keep our person to the way we address a child on a street or put a motion. Yesterday I attended a funeral. The children of the street crowded about the hearse. The minister noisily said, "Get out of here, you kids." The policemen stepped forward, and without a word, but with a smile and arms wide spread, motioned them backward. The line faded. It brought to mind the scene when the disciples forbade them; but Jesus said, "Suffer the little children to come," and there was much more expressed in the way He said it.

SEEKING A WIDER AUDIENCE

The preacher's first task after his education and location will be his relationship to the public to whom he must address his appeal. The church provides him with a limited constituency of saints, but if this be all, his voice will not extend far. He will speak over an already too heavily laden party line. The press will be delighted to meet him, particularly if he follows a few simple rules, which any cub reporter will explain to him, about preparation of copy. Names, and photographs in a gloss finish, are always news. The high schools and Parent Teacher Associations and service clubs and lodges are always on the lookout for speakers with interesting material, and they will even tolerate a presentation of the gospel if one has common sense and does not talk "too good." Political party groups, the community chest, and other churches, and the undertakers, will all afford avenues of cultivation.

One often wonders how John the Baptist got his first audience. A voice is of little value unless it can be heard. The organizations within the Church can each be utilized as an agency for extending personal invitation. The building of competitive programs is of doubtful ethical value. We are building a kingdom and not a congregation. Of what value is it to remove a stone from one wall in the temple only to put it in another wall already near completion. Preaching is not bidding at an auction sale against our brothers. If the last religious census of the United States means anything, there is still within our parishes a clientele of more than fifty per cent, to be found and won for Christ. If we steal sheep from our brethren, we have not gained anything for anyone, least of all ourselves. The organization of new units of work will sometimes attract new attendants: a Tuesday Club for employed girls; a Boy Scout troop; a Junior robed choir; a World Wide Guild for adolescent girls studying missions; a mothers' club; a sewing society; a dramatic group; a band of King's Daughters; an organized men's society; a bowling league; a personal workers' group, who go each Sunday night to rural churches where there is no minister; an Americanization group, who meet in friendly fashion with the aliens in the neighborhood. All of these and many more will be feeders to one's congregation.

In getting a new constituency one must never lose the old, that is to say, those who are already on the field. Yet here is a danger rarely recognized, even by veterans. The loyalties to which you come in a new field are all with the former pastor. His retirement or removal has canonized him. Therefore, be conciliatory! Do not try to change all the church by-laws the first year. Establish friendship first. Prying is the meanest trait of a new minister and deserves the punishment it usually receives. It is indicative of a meddlesome spirit. Life does not often move forward upon constitutions written upon paper. It moves forward in good will. When the church members perceive that you are anxious to tinker with the by-laws, they think no better of you than they should. You have found their old ways not to your liking, and you are taking an unfair advantage of them in trying to have your own way. They succumb to your wishes with a mental evasion and bide their time. They know your day is coming. How much better to go on awaiting your time until good will and confidence are established. Usually the church will respect the pastor more who tries to force nothing through, and who in business meeting allows the business men to lead the way. If he is in the chair and the vote is likely to be closely divided and indecisive, he may say, "Brethren, I would very much prefer, with your consent, not to put this motion, if the maker of the motion will consent. And I think if we wait for a week or a month and talk it over together in that time in the spirit of prayer, we may reach a unanimous decision. Let us pray." I have never but once seen such tactics fail to achieve unity. Love and prayer are better than all the by-laws in the world. Christian men rarely call for a quorum. It is always good parliamentary usage to act like a Christian. Do not rush into the denominational press, telling the world that in the first three months of the present pastorate, the deacons have been obliged to drop one hundred names of members who could not be found, but that in spite of this, the congregations have increased three hundred per cent. Your predecessor was a godly man. He did his best. The people who are now cultivating you, made his life a burden without reason. Your turn with them will come too. Make to yourself friends for that day by your conduct now. Be fair to your confreres.

THE EXACTING PRICE OF LEADERSHIP

"Ye have been bought with a price," says Paul. Yes, and in making transfer of the purchase to the One who redeemed us, we pay an exacting price too. We are not our own. We give over to Him and to our congregations a well body, an informed mind, a dedicated spirit, and all our time, thought, talent and treasure.

BODILY EXERCISE IS PROFITABLE

An exceptional servant of God, like Paul, may do good work with a "thorn in the flesh," but it will not excuse us for diminished nervous energy which we could prevent by self-denial; nor for irritation which we could avoid by temperance; nor for a husky voice which we could eradicate by diaphragm control.

In spite of the fact that William Cowper was of unsound mind, yet could sing "God moves in a mysterious way his wonders to perform," God will perform better through us in a sound mind! Pope sought to "justify the ways of God to man" and lived in a straight jacket all his life. But Beecher was the better saint, who could both preach of muscular Christianity and exemplify it. The preacher who can hike, and swim, and ride, and catch a ball, and play a game of golf just under one hundred, will be a better preacher because of it, provided he is not the slave of any of these, but keeps everything in its proper proportion. Paul told Timothy to take care of his body. Jesus lived a simple, healthy life, as a carpenter. The body that was nailed to the cross was a healthy body. All through the New Testament, in spite of asceticism, the body is glorified. "The flesh" is the symbol of sin and of our sinful nature. But "the flesh" is a different thing from the body. "The flesh" is *not* sound nerves, and muscular tissue, and prompt accurate reflexes. "The flesh" is drunkenness and the Saturnalia, and over-feasting, and eroticism, and all those sins against which Paul warned the Galatian Christians: fornication, wrath, strife, and revel. These are physical but they are the physical beast out of control. They have the trainer down and are clawing him.

It is a different physical side that we see at games. There

the body is coordinated to its maximum. This figure of the contender at the games Paul loved. "Gird up your loins . . . quit you like men, be strong." "Glorify God in your body," said Paul, and stopped there. It was a later gloss that added, "and with your spirit." That was added when men began to be afraid to be clean and strong for Christ. The abuse of the body is post-apostolic. Health is consistent with the genius of early Christianity.

It was the year 397 A.D., four centuries after Christ was born, before Simeon Stylites treated the world to the piteous and disgusting spectacle of a man covered with ulcers and vermin, scorched by the sun by day and pinched by the frost by night, who spent the last forty-seven years of his life atop a ruined pillar, dependent for food upon the pilgrims who visited his "saintliness." There he sat astride his pillar without privacy of any sort. He supposed that he was growing a great soul for the Kingdom by such mortification of the body. Perhaps the angels turned their noses at the odorous carrion who thought himself holy, and who was only dirty and queer.

There are special strains that fall upon the minister's body. His nerves must always be in perfect control. He must never be seen out of temper. He must never show irritation at the constant succession of maddening nettle stings, administered by ignorance and envy and pique and revenge, that torture a sensitive soul. These are the sandflies of religion. There are even those who will take especial delight in goading us to fury just before we ascend into the pulpit and who will practice every wile to contact us immediately before the holy office for the joy of seeing us writhe under their verbal castigation. They will play upon our fears, our ambitions, and even our repressions. We will need a good body to endure this.

TIME OUT TO KEEP HEALTHY

We are in need of longevity. It takes a long time to bring things to pass. Disembodied spirits are destined not to do much in this life except in ghost stories. Charlotte Bronte and her sister would have been happier saints if their lives had not been shortened by tuberculosis. It takes time to outlive those who are opposed to us. Our very best success will come from keeping alive. Time is an acid that eats away all difficulties. Longevity and good behavior are our two best assets.

Health must help us to retain youth in old age. We must feel young no matter how old we are. A healthy person will not be nearly so inclined to become morose. Froude says, "Erasmus didn't get into hot water but he certainly made the water hot for all about him." The minister must not be a valetudinarian, always thinking about his health, always speaking of it. That in itself is a disease. The healthy organ is the organ concerning which we are not conscious. "No news," concerning my body, "is good news."

A public speaker on health said, "If you wake at night to find that you are breathing through your mouth, get up and shut it." Our pores must be open, our skin deodorized. Our teeth must be clean and our breath sweet and free from offensive odors. Without passing upon the conventions of society, criticising our brethren who are as good or better soldiers than we, making ourselves saints because we are troublesome, we would say this good natured word: tobacco is still objectionable to many excellent people. There is no more reason to smell of it than there is to smell of onions or garlic or any other odorous substance. If we use it, we must also use the tooth brush, and not carry fumes to those whose noses will be offended.

Let us take time for our toilet, and face the world clean. Let us take exercise but avoid athletics. The daily rule for the preacher, to be followed religiously, should be: "Exercise, bathe, shave, dress." Play every day. Let the well body help you to smile in the face of any emergency or task.

BE KIND TO YOUR VOICE

The most interesting discovery I ever made about my own preaching was this: The state of my health affects the quality of tone or timbre, as the musician would say, of my voice. And this in turn directly affects my audience. A high pitched tone makes an audience irritable, fearsome and edgewise. A habitually high-pitched voice gives the same impression to an audience that one has who hears a female child in distress or complaint, and can do nothing about it. A middle pitch is the tone of faith and quiet friendliness. A low pitch is the most difficult to sustain and is the natural medium for solemnity. I usually pick out a person on the back seat and imagine myself talking to him. An annoying tickle in the throat can be relieved usually by clearing the back of the nose, or by opening the throat consciously with chin upraised, as if one were about to gargle. These movements may all be performed while speaking and without attracting attention to one's self, by the use of care. If the throat goes into a spasm, as every speaker knows it may, keep your head, go slowly, breathe deep, and smile.

I love to sing, but I rarely do. I follow the tunes with my congregation in a speaking voice, and no one is the wiser. The muscles one uses in speaking are not those one uses in song. Few men can both speak and sing. Thank God if you can. Most of us cannot.

PREPARED FOR SICK CALLS

One should have a healthy body for the visitation of the sick. How can a priest refuse any call upon his sympathies? The telephone rings. He does not say, "Is it contagious?" He goes. He remembers the assurance, "and these signs shall follow them that believe; in my name shall they cast out devils; they shall take up serpents; and if they drink any deadly thing, it shall not hurt them; they shall lay hands on the sick, and they shall recover." Jesus was not telling us to be imprudent. But he was giving mental assurance to the man who must go among the sick. Health is infectious. It makes us immune. The pneumonic child coughs and the air is laden with germs. The doctor must visit that room and so must we. Let us prepare for that visit with health. Let us preach at least one eloquent sermon to that afflicted houschold by the fearless cheer with which we stand by when our influence counts most.

Theodore Roosevelt was told by his physicians that he could not live, when he was a very young man, and when he had been hopelessly defeated by ward politicians in New York City. He went to a forlorn spot in the Dakotas and won back health and vigor, and lived to defeat his detractors and became a great president. Remembering that story, one pastor, during the influenza epidemic of 1918, said to the nurse at the call desk, of the City-County Hospital, "If you need a Protestant pastor, I will come at any hour of day or night."

He was the Father Damien for the city of half a million, and his quiet confidence silenced the mad hysteria of fear that gripped the community and that was worse than the disease. He too had known what it was to be so low that he could look into the grave. Having seen, he was not afraid.

MAN'S EXTREMITY, GOD'S OPPORTUNITY

Here is a personal experience, sent me by a friend, concerning the pastoral call upon the sick.

"When I was seventeen I was very ill and I did not know Christ. My heart was as black as the pines on cemetery hill at twilight, and fear oppressed me. The doctor came and said to my mother, 'Madame, I have done all I can. You are at liberty to call in any other physician.'

"Outside I could hear them talking. My father said in a low voice, 'but when will he die?' I strained my ears and the physician said, 'Physically speaking, he is as good as dead already.' Then my mother sent for the minister. I had turned my face to the wall and was weeping bitterly. On the wall was an old scroll, reading, 'Forasmuch as ye know that ye were not redeemed with corruptible things as silver and gold from your vain conversation . . . but with the precious blood of Christ.' I tried to pray, but I couldn't. By and by the minister came. He brought me a crimson carnation. He asked me how I felt. He complained of the congregation Sunday. He scolded about the unfair methods of another church. He told me he loved me and wanted me to drive his horse for him when I was well again. And he patted my head and smiled and went away. And I groaned in spirit as he went out the door. I wondered if he really knew Christ. The next day the weather was terrible, but my former pastor drove eighteen miles through the blizzard to see me. He came directly to my bed. He took my hand. He said, 'Lad, when I came by the lake just now, there was a thick cloud hung over it, and its depths looked sad like your poor heart. Your mother and I are praying for you, boy. We want you to live. But first, we want you to accept the Christ of the motto there.' And I broke into weeping again as I asked, 'Do you think He'll accept me?' And very wisely going to the heart of the matter, he said, 'I know. "Him that cometh to me I will in no wise cast out." Will you come now?' And I said, very simply but with all my heart, 'I will and I do. For life or death, I come.'

"And before I knew it, he was on his knees on one side of my bed, and my mother was beside me on the other, and he told Jesus of Lazarus, who came to life at the Savior's tears, and he quoted Kingsley: 'Thy tears shall raise to life His frozen limbs again.' Even while he was praying, the sun came out, and I felt an assurance that I should live, for my work for Christ had just begun. The stone rolled back from the tomb, and it was my resurrection morning. I knew that day what a pastor's call should be like. I knew that I had passed from death unto life, for His mercy's sake."

HOW WELL DO WE KNOW THE HOMES

We promote peace of mind for ourselves and others by our general pastoral calls. Remember that Jesus was the first one to say that social relationships bear a direct relation to the spiritual life. "If thou bring thy gift to the altar, and there rememberest that thy brother hath aught against thee; leave there thy gift . . .; first be reconciled to thy brother, and then come and offer thy gift." John confirms this, "For he that loveth not his brother whom he hath seen, how can he love God whom he hath not seen?"

If we have a church, let us call in every home and know every member during the first year. Repeat that annual visitation regularly. Let no overlaying of heavy burdens or social entanglements prevent it. One must not neglect it.

Ten calls per day should be the minimum, five days per week. My own experience is that for every fifty calls, I get one new member. There are many homes where one will be as welcome at nine A.M. as one will be from two to five, but care must be exercised. Monday is the day to see the old, the sick, and the chronic shut-in. Saturday may seem impossible. But this is the day in which to see the unevangelized, the disinterested, the disaffected, and the awakened. Such calls should be very limited in time. "You know how busy I am today. But I could not let the day go by without seeing your face and telling you of the prayer in my heart. Tomorrow I shall hope to see you." A pat on the shoulder and you are gone. Births, deaths and social occasions must be respected. These are deep moments when indirect preaching is always most eloquent. A moment ago we put on the lips of the pastor the expression "busy." It is a word he will rarely use. It is a non-conductor. It builds a barrier when a person says, "I did not call you, pastor, because I knew how busy you always are." You may know that they are either tactless or ill-natured. The only permissible retort, when one adopts that tone, is quietly to reply with a smile, "But *never* too busy to see special friends like you."

There are always the pests who waste our time. I see no way to avoid this. With the grace of a Chesterfield, they must be shown the door and left outside, thinking they got there themselves. Sometimes it is possible to make a special grace of walking arm in arm to the door with them. But no matter how tedious they are, we will never say contemptuously of them, "Raca" (Matt. 5:22), for Christianity has put a seal of worth on all souls, even these.

But there are time-wasters just as bad, for which we are

wholly responsible. Gerald Stanley Lee wonders how Jesus did so much and never served on a committee. Do not scatter your interests too widely. You must not be too busy to do each task well.

THINGS TO BE LEFT UNSAID

My mother forbade me, as a boy, to discuss at the table:

1. Diet.
2. Drugs, illness, operations.
3. Death.
4. Dementia and insanity, in any case whatsoever.
5. Anything disagreeable.
6. Duties and conduct of servants.
7. The dress and demeanor of people.

We might relate or discuss any informing circumstance of the day, or any interesting story we had heard. Our family was large and there was much happy conversation. As I think of it now, she guided us between the narrow rocks of idle gossip and ill-natured criticism into a calm sea of smiling observation. I believe she set certain standards that have often helped me. There have been moments when only the utmost attention has saved my naturally quick tongue from personal comment for which I would later have been sorry.

In conversation one should not monopolize. Few people talk too little. We are rarely sorry for what we do not say. Too much of even good talk is an evil. Drawing out our interlocutor is always safe and sometimes informing, or even rewarding. James says, "Swift to hear, slow to speak, slow to wrath."

PUT A KNIFE TO YOUR THROAT, WHEN HUNGRY

The preacher will watch his food, that it be nutritious, sufficient to repair waste tissue. The nourishing things are usually the inexpensive things. Two men went from America on a preaching tour of Europe. One spent for food twice as much as the other, and came home to die. He tried to get the food he was accustomed to here. When the second man was asked how he fared, he replied, "I always chose the cheapest meal on the menu." "Why?" "Because I knew it was the food of the largest number of native people. And for that reason I knew it would be best cooked and most sure to be fresh."

No one properly digests food eaten nervously. Be very sure that the way in which we are at ease when invited out, and blend easily into a situation, will determine whether we are invited again. And this will determine the sum total of the impression we are able to make upon some of our most influential parishioners. The Jesuits train their priests to be at ease in the presence of great wealth. Meditate on that when next you hear of the transfer of huge estates to the cause of Rome. The Oxford Group Movement members are at home among the well-to-do. Meditate upon that, too. Jesus was at ease in the house of Simon the Pharisee. When one thinks of it, He was always at ease when among the cultured.

THE MEMBERS OF MY CHURCH AND THEIR HUSBANDS

Two-thirds of our congregation will be women. Let us make it our business to know men where they assemble. Let us meet them with refined manners. Let the most obvious testimony to our office be found, not in special garb, which we may or may not wear, but in face, mind, speech, habit of thought. We will not advertise the gulf that already separates us. It will be only too apparent to others. The best dressed woman in all England when she visited Boston recently merged into the crowds of Tremont Street unnoticed! The best dressed people are not seen for their dress.

The points of one's person that will be noted most quickly will be the face and head, the neck at the hair line, and the extremities. The hair must be cared for sufficiently often, so that no one says, "I see that you've been to the barber." The face must be shaved daily and at the beginning of the day. Start the day clean.

THE DATE BOOK

One pastor, in his early ministry, thought he could carry all his dates in his mind. He forgot a dinner engagement in the home of his wealthiest member. He lost an influential friend. The loss was profitable to him. It taught him to keep a day book of engagements. It was his first and last lapse of memory. One should call both before and after a funeral. Let us call within a week after a wedding, or any other social function. Let us make our calls brief. Let no ordinary call last over fifteen minutes. In these days of automobiles, four calls per hour is the rule. It is sufficient for any pastorate, in village or city. You are not there for a visit. Your technique on such an errand is well defined. In the case of joy, it is to be blithe. In the case of sorrow, it is to let them see your sympathy. In the case of admonition or invitation or arrangement of functions, or acquaintance, one will come directly and happily to the point and leave promptly when one arises. A prayer is always a part of every visit. But it is not always expressed. It will be a prayer if you only say, "I love you and pray for you daily," or "God bless you," said not lightly, or the Levitical benediction or some New Testament phrase, "The God of peace keep you," or "I shall hold you up to God tomorrow morning at nine in intercessory love," in the case of an impending operation.

Greetings are always for the host first and good-byes are for the host last. When shaking hands let us not grip too hard. Pastoral calls are not a wrestling match. Last impressions are the more permanent. Say what you have to say, not only with a smile, but in such a manner as to convey your deepest interest in that person. You can undo all the good of your visit by a too hurried or a too long drawn out good-bye, or by a lack of the proper decorum.

CHAPTER VIII

ON WHAT SHALL I PREACH?

HE STALKED like Hamlet's ghost into my mind, and pointing an accusing finger at me Sunday night, after the first day in my first parish; he demanded, "What are you going to preach about next Sunday?"

"I preached today on the Cross," I said, "and next Sunday I shall speak lovingly of the One who hung upon it."

"And what," he continued, "is your theme for the Sunday after that?"

"The Church," I replied.

"And the Sunday after?"

"Oh, I have my morning subjects all blocked out for a full forty-eight Sundays," I said.

"And what of Sunday nights? They will be the time that will test your soul's fortitude."

I was honest enough to tell him that I had not given the matter much thought. "You'd better," he said, "if you expect to hold your job!"

Now it was my turn, and I told him plainly and once for all that mine was "not a job," it was a "divine calling." "It doesn't make any difference to the flock," he replied, "you must deliver the goods. And, take it from me, young man, you have to think still further. You must not only have forty-eight morning sermons for the saints, and forty-eight evening sermons with catchy titles for the sinners, but you have a men's class to teach. You must prepare for it, and the lesson helps will not help you much. And you have at least forty-eight prayer meetings to lead. You will very shortly be like the country fireman faced with a conflagration and the well running dry."

"But I thought that a heart surrendered to the will of God would cover all that," I said. "It will help," was his only answer.

He left me that night, but not for long. He has haunted me and tortured my days. He is the ghost that will not down. I, like Paul, in all honesty of purpose resolved to know nothing among them "save Jesus Christ and him crucified." And I have stood "in weakness and fear, and in much trembling," and my most frequent prayer has been that "I might speak boldly so as I ought to speak." But repeatedly he has said, "You will preach the Cross! But how? Can you lead the sheep to the stream without muddying the waters? Is there an inherent depth to the well so that it gives forth living water? Is there enough in the Christian message to keep one's mind busy two or three times weekly for a life time?"

A woman was gone from her parish for a year. She returned to listen again to her pastor and went away with the biting comment, "and the evening and the morning were the same day."

The question we raise is not academic. It is partly a question of the content of our faith. "I believe in God the Father Almighty, Maker of heaven and earth, and in Jesus Christ, His only Son, our Lord; who was conceived of the Virgin Mary; suffered under Pontius Pilate; was crucified, dead and buried. He descended into hell. The third day He arose again from the dead. He ascended into heaven and sitteth at the right hand of God the Father Almighty; from thence He shall come to judge the quick and the dead. I believe in the Holy Ghost; the holy catholic Church; the communion of saints; the forgiveness of sins; the resurrection of the body; and the life everlasting. Amen."

Here are approximately six articles of faith. God, Christ, the Holy Spirit, the Church, the Forgiveness of Sin, and Life Everlasting. They can be expanded into possibly twenty subjects. But twenty subjects after all are not fifty-two. What shall we speak on for the rest of the year? Is it possible that the reality of this question has driven some ministers to topical preaching, and others to an exposition of the latest popular books, and others to pictures, and still others to an observance of special Sundays when patriotic and fraternal organizations are asked to grace the service? These things of course will replenish the cup. But they are at best only expedients.

Paginini might play to a great audience on but one string. But can the minster do this? Moody had a repertoire of a bare four hundred sermons and rarely exceeded a selection of one hundred. But he was an evangelist who went from city to city. He once said, when visiting Harvard University, that he could not exceed three weeks in one place with profit. But think of the men who go on for thirty years in one field, yet who keep fresh and new. How is it done? Are there more foci to the ellipse of the gospel than these, the Cross and the Resurrection? That the question is vital is testified to by Henry Sloane Coffin's resourceful and suggestive volume *What to Preach,* and by the equally remarkable book, *Jesus Came Preaching* written by Dr. Coffin's able successor, Dr. George Buttrick of Madison Avenue Presbyterian Church in New York City.

One young cleric found an answer to this query. He bought a cheap large print copy of the King James version and began to read with a pencil in his hand and a notebook by his side. That notebook has expanded until it completely fills two large steel filing cabinets and that inexpensive copy of the Bible has become his most precious possession. Every preachable text in it has been marked and catalogued and analyzed and filed with cross references. He has read the book through, not as a slave of literalism, but as an artist might visit the European galleries or the Athenian Acropolis, to come close to the fount of inspiration. He has preached twice every Sunday for thirty years, and his latest sermon bears the number 3,936, which means that he is still writing at least two new sermons every week, and has lost any expectation of preaching himself out. The human mind offered to Christ is an inexhaustible reservoir. Unlike a vein of silver in a mine, it never "peters out."

He resolved to test his own heart. He first of all went back over all his seminary material. He took the fields successively of Hymnody, and Missions, and Church History, and Doctrine, and Homiletics, and Sociology, and tabulated the subjects upon which a church should be made aware. But he remembered that he faced the danger of being pedantic, and of separating preaching from reality. He prayed, "God help me to keep the pulpit and the pew near neighbors." His criterion was always Christ. He started a clipping file of stories, illustrations, quotations, and choice sermon titles. He read no book without giving it careful analysis, tearing off huge steaks and hanging them up in his wigwam to cure.

Concerning stories he made this rigid requirement: they must be personally applicable and not far-fetched. One of the greatest fields of human interest in the church was its school.

He began to investigate and interpret this in the light of the child that was gathered in the crook of Jesus' arm. He examined problems that vex that major institution: the parent, the teacher, the child, the curriculum, the Christian decisions, the indelible stamp, the officiary. He sought to find what light the gospel shed, what principles might be derived from the Great Teacher. He began to ask, what is there in the gospel of human interest? Where do truth and interest hold their secret tryst? May I have the joy of wedding the two?

PREACH BIOGRAPHY

The subjects which have made the *American Magazine* one of the best sellers will appeal to the hearts of church attendants. They like to hear of men who have "gone places" and "done things." A congregation never tires of sermons on the lives of great heroes, martyrs, missionaries, and apostles of the church. Let the minister, then, give a series of sermons on biography. The lives of the Old Testament saints are full of dramatic spiritual quality: Moses, David, Elijah, Daniel, "of whom the world was not worthy." And then there are the terrible failures: Esau, Samson, Absalom and Saul. And there are the great women of the Old Testament: Deborah, Abigail and Hannah. The story of these puritan maids of another epoch fairly point their own moral. Eveleen Harrison's two books, *Little Known Women of the Bible* and *Little Known Young People of the Bible* are splendid volumes suggestive of this development.

And here within three verses of each other are Tamar, Rahab, Ruth and the wife of Uriah, all included in the genealogy of Jesus. A man would be dull who could read those names and not find a sermon, especially if he finished the chapter, and read, "Thou shalt call his name Jesus, for he shall save his people from their sins." In the New Testament is "the glorious company of the apostles," with Paul. And friends whose life Jesus touched, Lazarus, Zaccheus and Nicodemus; each of these deserves a sermon.

PREACH ETHICS

In the morning services, one might well run through Paul's list of the fruits of the Spirit in Galatians 5, or at least hang them all on one golden thread. He will make an evening series on the seven deadly sins: pride, envy, gluttony, lust, sloth, anger, covetousness. He will not dilute the dose. He will be honest and straightforward. These subjects all have a sharp edge. He must hew to the line. Now, when ethical standards are low, is the time to preach a series on the ten commandments, to find if we have here the announcement of abiding values. And concerning those ten commands the most fruitful question he will ask is this: *why* were they given? They are not arbitrary and meaningless. There is pragmatic insight behind them. And if so, does that ethical principle still abide, or are these words merely for an interim. It is his answer to that question, "*Why* the ten commands?" that will make the series live. Follow such a series with the Beatitudes, first as a whole, and then taking up each one separately.

PREACH DOCTRINE

The world is hungry for the doctrinal sermon again and the entire group of divisive teachers are up stage shouting their lines. Preach on God, and Christ, and the Holy Spirit, and the Atonement, and the Cross, and Sin, and Faith, and Conversion. He will write a sermon for men and preach it to them only, their habits, their motives, their especial dangers, their longings which none but a man may know, their salvation.

Interpretations of Jesus are always listened to. His life is the matchless miracle. With Him Christianity was a fact. He lived it. He lived it in a day when nothing in the social history of the day prepares our hearts for His coming except the blackness of the night. Yet prophets sang of Him. Their faith read the heart of God aright. "Who hath believed our report, and to whom is the heart of the Lord revealed?" I do not wonder at the story of the Virgin. Men had to have some reasoned explanation for such as He. I wonder that men doubt it. This was not just another. This Babe is the authentic word. In Him God speaks. If man can save me, let me go on the street and pick anyone. But if only God can save, let me pause in divine amazement before this cradle. There is something here the world has waited for. It has never seen the like before. It will never see His like again. That wonder still stands. Of every genius it must always be said that he grew up "as a root out of a dry ground." In Jesus' case it is preeminently true that His nation, His age, His church, His relationships and His environment do not explain Him. He is like the priceless orchid that nourishes itself directly from the air. He is still, as Lanier said, "The Crystal Christ." The last verse of that poem is one that *must* be memorized.

I do not find the Greek creed-makers satisfactory for my day. But what they said for their day I should like to say for mine.

"God was in Christ, reconciling the world unto himself." "Seeing it is God that shined in our hearts, to give us the knowledge of the glory of God in the face of Jesus Christ." "And the Word was made flesh, and dwelt among us, (and we beheld his glory, the glory as of the only begotten of the Father,) full of grace and truth."

PREACH TO WOMEN

He will speak at remote intervals to women alone. The greatest text in the Old Testament for woman is Proverbs 31, but the stories of Ruth and Esther and the wife of Hosea are not to be passed by. The greatest text for women in the New Testament is Luke 13:12. What is it from which Christ has loosed woman during the centuries? Loosed in body, mind and social customs, what folly and wickedness it would be if the freed woman does not arise to glorify God like her ancient sister. The three worst wives in history are Xantippe, Mrs. Wesley, and the wife of Job. Preach on this nameless, fair-weather wife of Job, who bade her husband "curse God and die." Let her be the background over against whom you paint Lois and Eunice and all their train (II Timothy 1:5). No wonder our churches are filled with women when we consider what Christ has done for her since the days of Claudia, the saintly wife of Pilate.

In similar fashion deal with the child. The entire burden of childhood comes upon the parents so unexpectedly and heavily, and is passed on so quickly and leaves such bitter regrets when it is lifted forever, and our knowledge in this field is so experimental and shadowed by so much of bigotry and superstition, that the pastor must speak his mind here. Who even yet takes seriously this text: "their angels do always behold the face of my Father," or "except ye be converted and become as this little child." What is the child's place in the field of training? Has the One who was born a babe in Bethlehem and who announced His relationship to God at the age of twelve no contribution to make to our thought? Can we only sit supinely by and watch the blood stream wreak more havoc than the Ohio and Mississippi and all their tributaries? Or has Christ a valid word as much to be listened to as Froebel or Pestalozzi or Montesorri or John Dewey. If Christ has such a word, what is it?

IF A MAN DIE SHALL HE LIVE AGAIN?

Death and Eternal Life are still vital questions. It is not Saint Chapeau and the sacred cause of millinery which crowds our churches on Easter but a deathless hope. Men are entitled to know, honestly, what Jesus and Paul said and experienced in this field, and to know how all our hopes are backed by reason, history, philosophy, science, morality and religion. They will be interested to know the five pictorial Greek words used in the New Testament to describe death. A breaking of camp (Phil. 1:23), a departure on a journey (Luke 9:31), an embarking on a boat (II Tim. 4:6), a sleep (John 11:11), an entering into another room (John 14:1), each one deserving a sermon. In what sense may these figures be used of death? Does identity continue? What of an intermediate state? Do the dead come back? With what body do they carry on? How are heaven and hell to be interpreted? Is there a great gulf fixed that can be spanned only in the present life and then by a cross?

Is Universalism, which has become well-nigh universal, a safe doctrine for either faith or ethics, as it is held by the average man of the street? Does science seem to teach it?

One will recall the Quakeress, who said to the visiting clergyman who applied for the pulpit and who announced the "larger hope": "If what thee says is true, we do not need thee, and if what thee says is not true, we do not want thee." J. Y. Simpson has something to say to us in his *Man and the Attainment of Immortality*. If the 15th chapter of First Corinthians and the 5th chapter of Second Corinthians are the two greatest chapters in the Bible on death, what is a true exposition of them?

Men like Leslie Weatherhead are frankly on the side of the ultimate triumph of the love of God, in a modified universalism. Another man, equally learned, commits himself to the doctrine of conditional immortality. Still a third rejects immortality, as such, as a pagan philosophy, and asserts that Christ's promise is of everlasting life, which is a qualitative thing beginning now. One cannot let these divergencies pass without notice. Men are hungry to know what the gospel says about the hope of life everlasting.

YOUTH

The young people have always loved the service when they have been permitted to choose one of their number to stand in the pulpit and ask straightforward questions quite fearlessly, and they expected and were granted the utmost of honesty in the answers. Such a service should be carefully thought through beforehand.

There was a time when every pastor loved the unusual or

freak text. "Alexander the Coppersmith"; "Aaron's Beard"; "Peter's Wife's Mother"; "Old Shoes and Clouted Upon Their Feet"; "Gravel-stones"; "The Nether Millstone"; "The bed is shorter than a man can stretch himself on it." Most of these are no longer in good taste.

The custom seems to have started with Origen. Thank God we've seen the end of it. Yet occasionally one will find an unusual verse that may be used if one frankly says, "I use this accommodatively," for example: I Samuel 19:2, "Take heed to thyself until the morning, and abide in a secret place."

It is possible to take some of the most commonplace expressions such as "come to Jesus," and ask just what we mean by these time worn expressions. Are they threadbare, like a worn out garment, or are they the tissue that covers a living frame?

It is possible to take the problem of suffering and interpret it in the light of the cross. John S. Whale of Cambridge, the brilliant youth recently chosen for an English college presidency, and E. Stanley Jones, and several others, have each written on some phase of this subject and their books have had a large sale. Evidently it is a live subject.

The man who can face his congregation as a convinced optimist in the face of evil is in a stronger position to assist struggling burdened souls than the one who still finds himself in the shadow. There are three great texts that should go together. "The steps of a good man are ordered by the Lord: and he delighteth in his way. Though he fall, he shall not be utterly cast down: for the Lord unholdest him with his hand." The second is from Paul, "All things work together for good to them that love God, to them who are the called according to his purpose." The last is the believer's bank note, a blank check on the vaults of heaven, signed by a solvent partner, who leaves the amount a blank to be filled in, in accordance with the need of the holder. That verse reads, "My God shall supply all your need according to his riches in glory by Christ Jesus." That triptych of hope deserves a series of three sermons. No one will preach them, however, until he has come to honest terms with them. If they are true, it is much to say so.

BOOK REVIEWS? NO!

Book reviews in general are to be eschewed unless they can be made quite definitely the basis of a presentation of the grace of God. Luccock is one of the very few who have been able to do this. The old lady was right who accused her perennial book reviewing parson of having been graduated from the Bible into the almanac.

PREACH THE BIBLE

"Gold is where you find it." One would never guess that it is in the Sacramento valley, but the gold dredges there are taking out a reported $15,000 per week. Sermons are where your heart finds them. John 3:16 will be rock ballast to a tired mind, and the first chapter of Chronicles will glisten with ore to another. Books, papers, magazines, the world-movement, daily events, experience, all afford an inexhaustible field, but chiefly *the* Book, because in its essence it is a comment on religious reality. It produces its best yield when read not to confirm creed or opinion, but to see life clearly and whole.

Let us take the most difficult book but one, in the entire sixty-six, Genesis. Tabulate for yourself as you read, pencil in hand. After you have made your first outline read McFadyen's *The Use of the Old Testament* to see what he would have done.

It does not matter what your religious angle. Come at the incidents as an honest man with a passion to translate the religious experience of yesterday into the experiences of today. G. Campbell Morgan has done it conservatively. Raymond Calkins has done it for the book of The Revelation from the modern angle. You are entitled to do it for yourself and your people in your own way. Here is a partial list of what one man found in Genesis, picking up only the headlines.

I. THE STUDY OF THE BOOK ITSELF

1. In outline.
2. Place in history.
3. Place in literature.
4. Place in field of morals.
5. Place in devotional life.

II. CHIEF CHARACTERS OF THE BOOK

(Studying trends in life)

1. Abraham.
2. Isaac—the son who reproduced his father's mistakes.
3. Jacob—a third generation Christian.
4. Joseph—an *American Magazine* prize story.
5. Sarah.
6. Rebecca—Lady Macbeth, 4000 B.C.
7. Rachel—origin of David Copperfield's Dora.
8. Dinah—the white slave traffic.
9. Hagar—the servant problem.
10. Lot—never pays to gamble.
11. Reuben—first born and a failure.

III. ISOLATED TEXTS

1. Good Earth, 2:7.
2. Brother's Keeper, 4:9.
3. Walking With God, 5:24.
4. Terah's Pilgrimage, 11:32.
   (He started his eternal quest too late in life—a sermon for youth).
5. Pitching One's Tent, 13:12.
6. God Led Me, 24:27.
7. A Fortune Wasted on Food, 25:34.
8. First Night from Home, 28:11.
9. Household Gods, 31:30.
10. When the Past Catches Up, 32:1.
11. Life Begins at 130, 47:8.
12. Shiloh, 49:10.
13. Ol' Man River, 2:10.
14. Unlucky Thirteen, 13:13.
15. God's All-Seeing Eye, 16:13.
16. A Text for Every Day of the Year, 32:26.

IV. GENERAL TOPICS

1. God, 1.
2. Sin, 2 and 3:5.
3. Prayer, 4:26.
4. Worship, 8:20.
5. Memory, 47:19.
6. Hope, 17.
7. Faith, 15:6.
8. Missions, 20:2.

V. STORIES AND INCIDENTS

1. Babel and Race Prejudice, 11.
2. Biography of a Business Man, 19.

3. Good Man's Mistakes, 20.
4. Choosing a Wife, 24.
5. Mother's Day, 27.
6. Mizpah, 31:49.

VI. PHILOSOPHICAL PROBLEMS

1. Evolution, 1:1.
2. Problem of Evil, 3:1.
3. How Rid the World of Evil, 7:1.
4. Literalism, 2:20 (contrasted with John 6:63).
5. The Omnipresence of God, 28:16.

VII. WORLD LIFE

1. Marriage and the Home, 2:24.
2. Woman, 2:20.
3. Labor, 3:19 (cp. 8:21 and Deut. 23:5).
4. City, 4:17 and 18:20.
5. Beginnings of Nationalism, 11.
6. Birth Control, 1:22.
7. Seventh Day, 2:2.
8. Dove of Peace, 8:8.
9. Drink, 9:21.
10. Unity, 11:1.
11. A Benevolent Dictator, 41.

VIII. SPECIFIC THEMES

1. Family Altar, 8:20.
2. Adversity, 39.
3. Tithing, 14:20.
4. God's Covenant, 15.
5. The Awareness of God, 15.

Here are sixty-eight sermon titles, actually tested out and proven good from a book often shunned lest it lead to painful controversy.

PREACH ON PRAYER

Cling to prayer as the one major interest of the midweek service. Live in the prayers of the Bible, and the men of prayer, and the experiences of prayer, ancient and modern, and the laws of prayer. We know one minister who has so faced every phase of the Lord's Prayer, and every prayer recorded from the lips of Jesus and Paul. Consult Andrew Murray's *With Christ in the School of Prayer* and Hallesby's *Prayer* for suggestive developments.

Prayer is the most productive agency of the Church. It can be revived. It is like the resurrection plant, that strange desert weed of the south-west. It dries up and blows away when water is lacking. It rolls before the hot wind over the dry sand, turning endlessly. But let it touch water! It unrolls lazily, puts down its roots, spreads its green, mossy leaves, and is alive again. It has found its complement. Prayer is the water of life to the soul. Our people would be profited by a rapid visualization of the experience of prayer in the life of Jesus. With the younger folk it might be made a project.

The Magnificat is prayer, Luke 1:47. The birth of John the Baptist was prophesied in prayer, Luke 1:10. Simeon's Nunc Dimittis is prayer, Luke 2:29. The highest point of Jesus' greatest sermon centers on prayer, Matt. 6:5-15. His Transfiguration, which even extreme modernists regard as a real experience, and which deserves study and interpretation, was born of prayer, Luke 9:28. His choice of disciples was made only after prayer, Luke 6:12; and is followed by an admonition for us to seek workers by the same method, Matt. 9:38. Demons departed when He prayed, Mark 9:29. Five thousand were fed when they heard Him pray, Mark 6. One of His beautiful brief prayers is preserved for us in Luke 10:21; a longer one in John 17. A prayer of concern for one he loved is indicated in Luke 22:32; the raising of Lazarus is said to have come at the close of a prayer, John 11:41; the cleansing of the Temple was in prayer, Mark 11:17; the breaking of the bread at the Last Supper was in prayer, Mark 14:22; the agony of the Garden, Mark 14:39, was endured in prayer; three of the Seven Last Words are words of prayer, "Father, Forgive," Luke 23:34; "My God," Matt. 27:46: "Father, into Thy hands," Luke 23:46. Does this sound like a multiplication table? Those who have tried it have seen it blossom like Aaron's rod.

The same thing has been done with the book of The Acts. Every triumphant experience of the early church, every victory over colossal forces that defeat us today, is a testimony to a living, working, present, personal God who works best for us by reason of our prayer. The gift of the Holy Spirit, Acts 1:14; the choice of Matthias, Acts 1:24; the conduct of the Church, Acts 2:42; the daily round of patient duty, Acts 3:1; the rejoicing in persecution, Acts 4:24-30; the death of Stephen which produced the conversation of Saul, Acts 7:55-60; the raising of Dorcas, 9:40; the conversion of Cornelius and the discovery by the Church that it must be world wide, Acts 10; the liberation of Peter's mind from bigotry in race and creed (10:9), and the surprising release of Peter from a prison cell (12:12); all are painted for us against a brilliant background of prayer. Prayer is even mentioned as a condition of salvation in Acts 8:22, and again it is a test in 9:11. It breathes in Paul's farewell address at Ephesus (20:36), and sustains a heathen crew in shipwreck (27:35). Imagination will make all of these scenes resplendent with action and color. Consult Canon Farrar for exactitudes.

The Epistles are full of prayer. The Epistle of James begins with instruction about prayer (1:5-8), and closes with the same admonition (5:13-18).

Moffatt translates I Peter 4:7, thus, "Steady then, keep cool, pray." That has sustained strong men when they knew death had them by the ear. Prayer must be habitual. And it must spring from holy desires. Think through the experience of Daniel. Marconi as long ago as 1907 sent a message 12,000 miles because of the perfect integration of the two instruments. The admonition to pray in the name of Jesus is not a counsel to empty formalism. It is a counsel to possess His Spirit.

Prayer must be offered in a forgiving spirit. Archbishop Hare in his Alton sermons vividly illustrates the way an unforgiving man really prays, "O God, I have sinned against thee many times; I have broken thy laws; I have committed many secret sins. Deal with me, I beseech thee, O Lord, as I deal with my neighbor. He hath not offended me one hundredth part as much as I have offended thee, but I cannot forgive him. He has been ungrateful to me, though not an hundredth part as ungrateful as I have been to thee, yet I cannot overlook such ingratitude. Deal with me, O Lord, as I deal with him. I remember and treasure up every little trifle which shows how ill he has behaved to me."

What does prayer do? Ask it as you read the story of the Syrophoenician woman (Matt. 15:21-28). Did she actually change the mind of Christ? Prayer, of course, does not change God's knowledge, or His love, or His purpose. But may it not make available to Him a heart through which He can act? The lights of Toronto proceed from dynamos which spin at Niagara Falls. When the lights went off, the falls were still running. It was the dynamo that had failed.

In our modern transportation, huge buses stop for a child when a finger is raised. Mechanics are geared to personality. Is it possible that God's vast creation is like that—that the universe responds to the cry of a soul?

Is it not time that we urgently counseled a return to the old forms again, prayer meeting, grace at the table, family prayer, and personal secret prayer? Have we not a duty to instruct our people in that old cycle of prayer that once every saint knew, beginning with adoration, thanksgiving, confession, petition, supplication, ascription, and waiting for the answer in humble trust, saying, "Not my will, but Thine?"

Sir Wilfred Grenfell gives as his testimony: "The privilege of prayer is one of my most cherished possessions, because faith and experience alike convince me that God hears and answers. I never venture to criticize; it is my part to ask; it is entirely His to give or withhold, as He knows is best. If it were otherwise, I would not dare to pray at all. In the quiet of home, in the heat of life and strife, in the face of death, the privilege of speech with God is inestimable. When I can neither see nor hear, still I can pray so that God can hear."

PREACH TEMPERANCE

Liquor has taken to our highways. Automobilists are concerned. Why not make a nation face the truth? It wanted liquor back. Does it want the wholesale homicide that liquor brought with it? Here is gambling. Has the craze for getting something for nothing, for striking a jack-pot, or winning the "sweeps," or putting up a quarter on Joe Louis because every one else in the office does so, any suggestive relationship to the soldiers who cast dice at the foot of the Cross? And here is the white slave traffic. The "strip-teasers" in the burlesque show are permitted in some of our cities. The relationship between gambling and drink and vice is very close and is often winked at in the city hall.

The movies are a marvelous invention. They are here to stay. It has been demonstrated that concerted action can persuade the pornographic impudence of producers in Hollywood. The preacher has a word to speak here. It must not wholly be one of denunciation. It must be a word of carefully measured praise.

The minister delivers many ephemeral addresses for special occasions. These, no doubt, will follow a well defined pattern. They will be brief; they will sparkle and be up to date; they will be congratulatory; they will be informing. Incidents of travel, and insights into everlasting principles of sound morality will be welcome if divorced from holy tones. A minister has a rare chance to sell himself and his gospel to various groups, but he must know his wares, and his life and speech must commend them.

THE FUNERAL SERMON

The funeral sermon is a problem. A prayer, a brief scripture, one that ends in an affirmation and not in the question mark of Job, and a brief homily, all lasting twenty minutes, will be enough for most services today without the hymns which are a variable matter of taste. Long ago I resolved that every service I held should follow the pattern of telling the truth, being kind and reminding the audience of its own mortality. Here, par excellence, is the place to be rid of notes.

One of our church school boys went with his grandparents

for the summer vacation. While away he died suddenly. They brought the body home and we held the service. I said the usual things. "God loans us our children. His fatherhood is more real than ours. He possesses His own. We know not now the why of it. We shall know hereafter. 'If ye loved me, ye would rejoice, because I said, I go unto the Father.' Life is richer here, and more certain there, because of the little traveler whom we have loved and lost, and whom we will meet when the day breaks and the shadows flee away."

After two weeks the parents sent for me. This is what they said, "Death was like a total eclipse. The sun was there, but it didn't shine for us. Your sermon was what we needed. It said what we knew but couldn't see. It was so good to have you say it to us until we came into the light again. Thank God you were not afraid to say the *obvious* thing."

Commit to memory Dr. J. H. Jowett's great utterance about death beginning, "Death is not the end," to be found in many service books, and see what it does for your mind at a funeral service, on one of those not rare occasions when you must fight to keep your own spirit from the hypnotism of another's grief. Do not use it slavishly. Let it be the tinder that lights your mind.

PREACH IN SERIES

Do not be afraid of sermon series. Preach through the Sermon on the Mount, and the Seven Churches of Asia, and take a vote of your people on the ten greatest chapters in the Bible and preach on that list. The most frequently chosen have been:

Psalm 23—God.

Isaiah 53—Christ.

Matt. 5—Ethics.
Luke 15—Man.
John 14—Faith and Prayer.
Romans 8—Applied Religion.
I Corinthians 13—Love.
I Corinthians 15—Death.
Hebrews 11—Faith and Heroism.
Revelation 22—Heaven.

Preach on the supreme moments of life: birth, death, marriage, and baptism, and face repeatedly the problems of Christian marriage and the Christian home, as for example, Husbands, Wives, Courtships, Home Piety, Reno, Companionate Marriage. Try to think with your congregation, of the Church, its aim, its origin, its officers, its ordinances, its marching orders, its perils, its hopes, its unity. Face the national problem fearlessly in the light of Sinai and Calvary. Many of these sermons should be textual or chapter or book expositions, but by no means all. Here is a series which might follow your visit to New York City. It is a series of five: Fifth Avenue and the Problem of Wealth; The Bowery and the Problem of Poverty; Broadway and the Social Evil; Ellis Island and our Alien Neighbor; The Churches and the Problem of Religion.

Your Jacob's Well will be inexhaustible. Neither the well of personal experience, which Jesus said would be a well of living water springing up into everlasting life, nor the well of the Book, will ever run dry. When one applies the gospel to the needs and interests of human life, one is reminded of the river of Ezekiel's vision. It began as a trickle under the steps of the Temple, but it broadened until it was a mighty river "that could not be passed through" (Ezekiel 47:5).

CHAPTER IX

PREACH ON THE CHRISTIAN HOME

Every year some time must be set aside to preach upon the *home*. There is no subject on which we must preach more honestly and persistently, nor with more restraint. If we do not reveal the ideals of a Christian home, the other sources of information are the modern, romantic, unreal novel, the cinema, the divorce court, the newspaper, the street, and the public dance hall. Can we believe that these give the desirable picture?

If high paid reporters on syndicate staffs answer letters from the love-lorn, and if the daily press finds such a feature essential, we may be very sure there is a sane demand for it. The demand is not psychopathic, but genuine, strong and wholesome.

We do not live in the Orient, where weddings are arranged within the clan by parents for a consideration. Here, mating time comes and we greet its mistakes with a sardonic grin, or with malediction, depending upon our temperament, or we say, "What is youth coming to?" Is there no one to say, that home you found may wreck society and you, or may be the anteroom of heaven? Is there none to say, that child you bear is an immortal soul whom God has loaned you to rear for Him and the Kingdom? Is there none to say sympathetically in the name of God, "the place whereon thou standest is holy ground"?

Courtship demands time and acquaintance and similarity of tastes, patience, and loyalty, on the part of the old for their young, trust on the part of the young for the old folk, and reverence between lovers themselves. It shuns jealousy which is love after it has soured. Love is not introspective, and engagements should not be long. When encouraged to do so, at such a service, young folk will utilize the question-box. This is always the time for greatest gentility. The following question is typical of a dozen handed in, in the course of a single evening. "I am engaged. Have been for over a year. We are drawing near to the time of marriage and I am getting nervous about it. I gave up a dandy boy with money, whom my sister wanted me to marry, because he seemed not to be a good Christian. It was all superficial with him. I am marrying a boy who is working in a garage, a hard worker, and a good business man, and a man who seems to think constantly about the fact that we are to have a Christian home and a family altar. What do you think are the big requisites for a happy home? I have been earning my own money so long that I am afraid I shall not be as economical as I should be, but I think religion will outweigh everything don't you? Am I doing wrong to marry when I feel any uncertainty?"

Back of every great life is a woman; Dante, Guido Reni, Browning, Disraeli, Garfield. Leonardo da Vinci's "Mona Lisa" is the eternal feminine, a problem even to herself. Many lives have been hurt by women, Socrates, Milton, Wesley, Dean Swift. The wife is always the "weaver" as the name indicates. The old German empress thought her relationship to her husband never transcended child, cooking, church, and clothes. What wife would be satisfied now with that horizon?

No woman looks to her man for money or wit. She looks for what she herself brings, character.

One might with propriety at a preaching service on the home recite the service, calling attention to its beauties and meaning. One would point out the most frequent pitfalls of married life: money, in-laws, the rearing of children, religion, unrestrained inherited temperaments, drink, sex. On the latter subject one will wisely refer them to a physician. One will counsel young people to make their home Christian, and to marry within certain broad religious lines which make for permanent happiness.

One will caution against expecting the impossible, and will urge health, love and character, as the great essentials. The Bible is rich in texts. There are the entire books of Genesis, Ruth, Proverbs, and Canticles; and Mothers Day, Fathers Day and St. Valentine's Day, and the month of June, all afford a time. In some such service one should bring into the pulpit Millais' "Angelus," telling its own story of love and labor and God.

The reason family prayer has waned is not that homes do not feel its need but that we have not pointed out the time and the way. The Methodist Episcopal Church, South, and the General Conference of the Methodist Episcopal Church have done a vast service with *The Upper Room*. It is one excellent agency to show the way. The evening meal is probably the acceptable hour with life geared as at present.

Let us be very sure that the permanency of the cause we serve depends upon the way we foster Christian faith in the home.

A woman sat by a hearth-side place,
Reading a book with a pleasant face,
Till a child came up with a childish frown,
And pushing the book, said, "Put it down."

Then the mother, slapping his curly head,
Said, "Troublesome child, go off to bed!
A great deal of Christ's life I must know
To train you up as a child should go."
    And the child went off to bed to cry,
    And denounce religion—by and by.

Another woman bent over a book
With a smile of joy and an intent look,
Till a child came up and jogged her knee,
And said of the book, "Put it down—take me."
Then the mother sighed as she stroked his head,
Saying softly, "I never shall get it read:
But I'll try by loving to learn His will,
And His love into my child instil."
    That child went to bed without a sigh,
    And will love religion—by and by.*

* Author and source unknown.

CHAPTER X

PREACH MISSIONS

AND why not? However we may define the word it signifies the principles and the design of the Founder of our Faith, and the method by which we have attained our growth. The question is not "Shall I preach missions?" but rather "How shall I present missions attractively and graphically? How shall I wed my people to a program that has always won? How shall I silence opposition that I know is born, not of ignorance but of ill-will? How shall I make men see Christ in relation to a world and to its crying need for redemption?"

One does not need to be a great theologian to discover in the gospels that Jesus believed profoundly six things. They are the heart of his message:

1. Every living soul, regardless of race or color, is precious in God's sight.

2. All men are equal before God.

3. Human life has limitless possibilities when linked to God, and any life, lost as it seems to men, may be redeemed.

4. The Christian enterprise is bound to succeed. It is a winning thing. It will not stop until it has conquered every frontier.

5. The principles and effects and relationships of the gospel will permeate all of life.

6. God's universe operates on the principle of God's redeeming love in Christ.

These six principles are the heart of all for which Jesus lived and died. They are as axiomatic as the multiplication table. Let us consider them separately.

First. Every living soul is precious in God's sight. The gospel has been translated into more than nine hundred languages and dialects. There is no record of any place where it has been presented from Greenland to Tierra del Fuego, from London to the Fiji Islands from the flats of the Yangtse to the ten thousand foot table lands of Thibet, that men did not tremble over sin, renounce their evil ways, burst into songs of faith, and die changed men when they accepted Christ. There are no favorites in the Father's house. "Doth he not leave the ninety and nine and go until he find it?"

Why should Christ love one man or race more than another because one has acquired sunburn from actinic rays while the other has not? Why should Christ prefer one man above another because one learned English and the other speaks Chinese? I do not treat my own children so. I loved my youngest when his only language was a cry, as completely as my eldest who was then already well advanced in school. I loved him as completely before he went to school as after he had gone for years. To be sure my companionship has been richer since, but my determination to perfect his personality, his character, and his usefulness, was just the same.

The sanctity of human life is the heart of the gospel. To look with contempt on any life is to part company with God. To be willing to die for men is God-like. "Greater love hath no man than this, that a man lay down his life . . ." The missionary movement as thus conceived is Jesus' plan of world salvation.

"How much then is a man better than a sheep?" is not a

proof text; it is a point of view. "Even so it is not the will of your Father which is in heaven, that one of these little ones should perish." It does not matter whether that life be Syrophoenician (Matt. 15:28), or Hebrew (Matt. 4:21), or Greek (John 1:43; 12:20), or Roman (Matt. 8:5; 9:18), or Samaritan (John 4:7).

Second. Jesus believed in the essential equality of all men before God. Ezekiel was perhaps the first to assert that "all men are created equal," but Jesus permitted no barrier to shut out a soul and its need. Perhaps it was this principle that came first with Him. Perhaps it is because men are equal in their essential soul quality that God is equally interested in them all. Certainly Jesus was equally interested in all men, whether He dined with rich Simon or reached out His hand to touch a leper; whether He conversed with Mary in a sheltered arbor of her wealthy home in Bethany or talked with an outcast Samaritan woman by a well curbing at Sychar. The point common to both the beggar, blind Bartimæus, who cried, "Have mercy," and the rich young ruler with pendant pearls on his velvet turban, who turned away, was that both had souls that were restless for God. The focus of attention for Zacchæus, the grafter, and for Nicodemus, who belonged to the elite intelligentsia, is at the point where both were seeking God and a better way of life. There is a point where all life meets: when it stands before God. This is the major insight that underlies Paul's great pronouncement: "All have sinned, and come short of the glory of God." It is not an ill-tempered, pessimistic, wholesale accusation hurled at men. It is a recognition that all men alike sense their need of God. Prince and pauper kneel at the gate. The parable of the workers in the vineyard, all of whom, at the end of the day, received a penny for their service, is Jesus' declaration that God has no favorites.

Third. Jesus believed in the limitless possibility of a soul that is linked to God. "This is life eternal that they might knew thee the only true God, and Jesus Christ whom thou hast sent." "The Son of Man is come to seek and save that which was lost." When Jesus looked down He saw no depth to which His arm could not reach to save, and when He looked up He saw no height to which He could not lift a redeemed life. Jesus is more than just the Saviour of a respectable man who needs no saving. He can save to the uttermost.

He saved Francis Thompson and Jerry McAuley and a nameless thief at Calvary. Bodies may be made over; ask any physician. Minds may be made over; ask any psychiatrist. Jesus went farther. "But that ye may know that the Son of Man hath power on earth to forgive sins, (he saith to the sick of the palsy,) Arise, and take up thy bed, and go thy way."

There have always been a few geniuses who, when walking the veldt, could see diamonds where others only saw a tedious gravel path. And there have been a few to see an alabaster city rising out of a wild onion swamp. And a few who could look at a starving Chinese boy dying on the hospital steps, and who could nurse him back to life and teach him of Christ until he became China's greatest statesman, who for at least five years has held Mars by the throat, almost single handed.

Missions is only another name for eyesight akin to the penetrating eyesight of the Christ.

Fourth. Jesus knew that the missionary enterprise He was establishing could never fail and would one day cover the whole earth. Success would come, however, as a gradual growth: "First the blade, then the ear, then the full corn in the ear." Neither would the success of the enterprise come without opposition and some failure along the path. "A sower went forth to sow . . . some seeds fell by the wayside . . . some had no deepness of earth . . . and some fell among thorns." Is not this parable applicable to the growth of the missionary enterprise too? Jesus was a realist. The movement He was founding must succeed. "When the Son of Man shall come in his glory, and all the holy angels with him, then shall he sit upon the throne of his glory." This verse is only one of the many indicating the thread of optimistic confidence running throughout his teaching. The Russian Soviet chant of youth, "We are making a new world," may easily have been adopted from our church hymn book: "Jesus shall reign where'er the sun doth his successive journeys run."

Fifth. The gospel of Jesus is not simply for the souls of men who are to die and who are to appear for judgment before a righteous God. It is the very gospel that must permeate all of life. "I am come that they might have life, and that they might have it more abundantly." "Ab unda," "Wave on wave." Life from God, as Jesus explains it, must be a surging tide that flows in and covers everything. The soul, the mind, the body, the home, the purse, social motives, the factory, the school, the place of recreation. Like His natural forces—air, light, vapor, heat, cold, wind, radio activity, electrons—God cannot be confined and He must permeate all of life even into one's innermost thoughts and motives.

Sixth. Jesus' philosophy was based upon an expanding universe. "God is love." The very essence of love is that it goes forever out and out, like sunlight redeeming the darkness of the night. If it drew in upon itself, it would not be love. If it were selective, loving only the lovable, it would not be love. Love never finds the burden heavy. Love never whispers, "I'm abused"; never grumbles, "I'm carrying more than half the load." It never suspiciously peers about to see who will get the credit for the deed. Never is it in a panic of fear or of self pity or of self-resentment, complaining, "They'll be sorry after I'm gone to see what they have done to me." Love often is lonely, but never too lonely. It has itself, and the dear unwitting, unworthy object of its adoration. Read again meditatively I Corinthians 13. All this is God as he pours out the golden store of His heart upon the world. All this is Christ as He staggers under His cross that His redeeming love may be the sacrifice for the world's salvation. And the very beauty of it is that love is never disappointed. Love is what the alchemist sought! It is the one magic reagent in all the world that actually purifies motives and does transform all things into likeness to itself. And so God can no more help being a missionary than He can deny His own Universe and its laws. If God be God, and if Christ be Christ, then Christ cannot live and die in Judea. God may be likened in His universe to the sun in the heavens; Christ may be likened to the evidence of the sun on our faces and on nature around us; and the Holy Spirit, God in action, may be likened to that unexplainable force of the sun that goes down into the earth, warms the seeds and forces all nature to grow.

You cannot explain the power of missions except through Jesus' great faith in God's redeeming love. Social revolutions, reforms, great upheavals have spent themselves in history and have given way to other movements, but the missionary enterprise is dynamic in its principles and purposes still. It cannot be stopped.

The missionary gospel is like a red hot iron. Lay it down

and try to forget it. It keeps on burning and consuming what surrounds it. "Do men light a candle and put it under a bushel?" Jesus was not admonishing us *against* hiding the light; He was telling us that if we have a light, we *cannot* hide it. Christianity itself is missionary, in spite of anything we can do about it. It shines forth. It discovers itself to men. The miracle of missions is that, in spite of our feeble attempts and the half-heartedness of our efforts, it refuses to die and is a vital force transforming the world in accordance with His promise.

Let us forget that strange concept which so many of us preachers seem to have—at least, judging from the sermons printed in periodicals—of a prepared address of well-sounding exhortation on the need for missionary work in Japan, China, Africa from the text Matthew 28:19-20, followed methodically by an annual offering for missions, vaguely conceived. A task that has been taken care of for the year!

You would never believe it, but it happened and it happened to me. I sat in a poor little church, and at the close of the sermon the minister said, "Now we're going to take a little offering for missions." His apologetic attitude prophesied the pitiful result.

Imagine, for illustrative purposes, what the cinema would do for patrons if the silver screen presented its great stories that way. The box-office receipts would tell the story. I am not advocating their methods for our purpose, but let us see if we can learn anything from them and from their successful achievement of drawing millions of people every day to spend, not a half-hour or three-quarters of an hour but two and three hours. Remember the effect upon the country of the stage production of "Rain" and its insidious influence upon our missionary work.

Pearl Buck, in her books on general subjects, has not painted a pretty picture of missionary work in China. Shall innuendo be met with silence; or honored and magnified by debate? Or does she yield her own secret of reluctant turning from a task that has now become painful, in this transparent story of her father and mother, so beautifully told but so poignant to read. It was brave, that life and service of theirs, and well meant unquestionably, but one wonders if a harvest has not at last ripened.

Missionaries are not meddlers. We need not be on the defensive. Our best answer is a more aggressive policy. Missionary societies will supply brochures on the lands and stations where your denomination operates. When done with these, other denominations will freely furnish excellent illustrative material.

MAKE PRESENT MISSIONARY PREACHING ROMANTIC

The great missionary heroes afford an inexhaustible reservoir: Raymond Lull, Francis Xavier, William Carey, Adoniram Judson, Ann of Ava, David Livingstone, David Brainard, John Eliot, Robert and Mary Moffatt, William Morrison, Henry Martyn, Francis Paton, Mary Slessor of Calabar, Dan Crawford, not to omit the gripping story of Grenfell of Labrador. The amount of space the secular press has devoted to Grenfell and to his work would seem to indicate that commercial interests sense the importance of his work of love and missionary zeal. The list is almost inexhaustible.

Basil Mathews has just published two inexpensive books. In *There Go the Ships* he gives the stories of Christopher Columbus, Vasca de Gama, Cook and others who sailed the seas for geographical expansion. In his second book, *There Go the*

Conquerors, he parallels the stories of discoverers with those of the great heroes of the faith who without gun, battleship, sword or shell "conquered" the world in His name. These books are worthy of our consideration and may help us to present missions more romantically.

The Moravian Movement should be studied in connection with Count Nikolaus von Zinzindorf and the historic site of Herrnhut. Hans Egede's life in Greenland is full of interest and instruction. The Boxer rebellion ties missions up with modern movements. Hearts still thrill to the story of Father Damien, making the discovery that he had contracted the contagion and speaking quietly the following day from the pulpit, "we lepers."

When one would preach the romance and adventure of Home Missions, think of those boys in your congregation who love adventure and are at just the age to enjoy James Fenimore Cooper's *Leather Stocking Tales.* Prepare for them carefully the story of the expedition of Meriweather Lewis and William Clark, who in 1805 extended our commerce to the Pacific Ocean, overland. Tell of Sacajawea, the immortal Indian maid, who piloted them through the gateway of the Rockies, negotiated with enemies, discovered paths where there were none, and taught them, when starving, to subsist on thimble berries. Listen to this from *Trails West.*

> "They had now reached the gateway of the Rockies. The scouts who had gone to the south came back reporting an impassable ravine. To the north lay miles of narrow ledges. To the rear were the blood-thirsty Sioux. Before them lay a deep lake of loveliest ultra-marine. The blistering sun came out and shining on the alabaster walls that

seemed to enclose them on every side, almost blinded them. Down the waterway they say a coyote, and above them soared an eagle.

'What shall we do?' said Clark.

'Listen to the maid,' answered Meriweather, sternly. As they were speaking already she had stripped the bark from an unusually large birch. She scraped the tender pulp from underneath and offered them to eat and ate herself. Then with their stomachs unsatisfied, upon this acrid and nauseating diet, they set to work, following her example, and in an hour had completed and launched a canoe. In this they set forth, closely hugging the shore and watching carefully lest over-hanging branches should capsize their craft. Toward late afternoon, by good luck and with the blessing of God, Lewis speared a land locked salmon weighing about seven pounds, and on this they broke their fast; yet even so making the fire ever so small and broiling the fish lest their presence might be made known to the Flatheads or the Nez Perce tribes ahead whose designs and friendliness they suspected. As they were about to lie down to rest, Sacajawea knelt, with eyes closed, and folded hands, then very solemnly she pointed upward and nodded her head three times. A faithful plainsman's wife had taught her of Jesus a year before, and the lesson was not forgotten. So committing her soul to God, she lay down, and was quickly asleep.

"In the morning, she was first awake, and gathered a large quantity of beech mast, which made a passable breakfast. Before they were allowed to eat, she looked at them and gently said, 'Gentlesmen, my God he get us troo. I guess you not know my God—huh—he best gentlesman ever live. Jesus, he my sheper', he get me good food, just like sheeps, he get Moses and chillanissel out worse mess an dis you bet. I tank my God, oh Jesu!'

"The whole recital had a profound effect upon both of the men and Lewis dropped to his knees. After they had risen from their knees Clark whispered to Lewis, 'What does she mean, chillanissel?' 'I don't know,' was the answer; but in the night Lewis awoke laughing with comprehension. He nudged Clark. 'She was talking about the children of Israel, you know, the Jews that Moses led out of Egypt.'"

Think of her when you see a hotel bearing her name in the far west. Think of her—"I guess you not know my God"—when you pray for a Christian America. America was won by souls like hers. Think of her when you sing, "O Beautiful for spacious skies." There are many other stories too which will help to present Home Missions romantically and graphically.

Consider Marcus Whitman in 1847. It will interest the boys in your congregation, and it will also interest their dads. You will no more hear, "The only good Indian is a dead Indian."

Four miles outside Palmyra, New York, is the hill of Cumorrah. Here the church of Jesus Christ of Latter Day Saints has erected a sign-board testifying that in the very year of which we have been speaking, 1805, a boy was born in Vermont, one Joseph Smith, who was also to have a part to play in the opening of the West. Here the Mormon Church testifies that the angel Moroni appeared to Joseph Smith and directed him to dig up plates of gold on which were written in Egyptian hieroglyphics, a revelation. Starting with this scene one might tell the story without malice up to the present moment. Think what the movies could do with that story.

Before preaching on India read Kipling's *Kim* and see what it adds of Asiatic color. Tell of the Philippines as a struggle story. See those people who wished to read the Bible now released from a penal code that forbade it.

If one would present the story of comparative religion what better than a resumé of Lewis Browne's *This Believing World,* or Alban G. Widgery's *Living Religions and Modern Thought,* or the story of Russia through the eyes of Maurice Hindus. What more vivid preparation could one find for preaching on Africa than Albert Schweitzer and his hospital at Lambarene.

The July issue of *The World* carries this item:

> "The Russian Government has decided, according to direct information from Europe to *The World,* to help spread atheism by official means and through official channels. Special attaches will be connected with Russian embassies and ministries in all foreign countries that have diplomatic connections with Soviet Russia, for the express purpose to stimulate the study of atheism throughout the world and to provide the means thereto. These attaches will be young communists, trained in one of the Godless Institutes in Moscow, and each one of them able to command several languages. The first of these attaches, it has been decided, will be sent to Mexico and Spain."

Who can keep Missions out of a sermon in a world such as that paragraph reveals?

One must tell the story of Alexander MacKaye of Uganda, who died aged forty-one, and of Chalmers, who when past sixty was eaten by cannibals in New Guinea in 1901. Think of that happening in this century! When telling of Arabia remember that Ion Keith Falconer died at the age of thirty-one. Four Christians names go with Arabia: Lull, Martyn, Falconer and T. E. Lawrence. The life story of each is fascinating beyond description. Make the date for such a service, June 30th, the date of Raymond Lull's martyrdom.

At least one romantic sermon should come out of the Pacific. Its discovery, its trade relations, its opium wars, coupled with the name of Warren Hastings; Hawaii, its Eden; the Philippines, its gateway to the Orient; its future, so gloriously certain, and the curtain of its stage just now rising upon Russia, China and Japan.

LET US REEXAMINE OUR BIBLE FOR TEXTS

The five classifications of books in which men are most interested are Travel, History, Romance, Adventure, and Biography. They are all wrapped up in one in missions. One would sometimes think, because of the constant use of them, that the only texts in the Bible on missions are Matthew 28:19 and Psalms 2:1. They have been overworked. But if one opens anywhere in Acts he cannot go wrong.

One might try Genesis 14:13, remembering that Abram was not a Hebrew until he left home, breaking all ties with the past, changing his nature, his name, his garments, his food, his language, his habits, and his religion. That is happening in India and China and Turkey today.

Here is Psalm 68:31. It tells of Afric's hope. Turn from

it to read of the Ethiopian eunuch and seek to put the story in modern dress. Let us remind ourselves that we must not overlook the possibilities of the books of Ruth and Jonah, those twin mission tracts. Resolve to have the luxury one Christmas Sunday of preaching a missionary sermon from John 4:4. Why must Jesus go into unpleasant alien territory, which Cook's agency would probably advise us to omit even today. No traveler visits Shechem that he does not speak of violence. Life is now as it was then in that hybrid center. His compulsion surely was not physical? What then? This is the continuing Incarnation of God in Christ.

The opening of Europe to the gospel began in the recorded facts of Acts 16. Examine Ezra and Nehemiah, and trace the exclusive tendencies of the Jewish faith which have been its modern undoing as a missionary movement. Look at Matthew 1: and remember that Rahab (Matthew 1:5) and Ruth were both foreigners.

One question constantly recurring in every missionary conference is that concerning the destiny of the non-Christian world. If they will be saved, why evangelize them? This must be answered. The answer is implicit in John 1:9 and Romans 2:14. Read with these texts, John 8:12 and Matthew 4:16. Coming to terms with a missionary policy was almost the first problem the Church faced. Read Acts 10.

HOME MISSIONS

Home Missions are often thought of as the "little end of the horn," an insignificant part of a great enterprise. Painstaking thought does not justify such a conclusion. The preaching of Home Missions is a great task by itself demanding especial and careful preparation. One must be fair to that great ecclesiastical organization, which is not Protestant, and mention Friar Marcos exploring New Mexico as early as 1539, and Marquette, Joliet, and LaSalle exploring the Mississippi from 1673 to 1682. One would also enliven the tale with Raleigh's efforts to found a Protestant state in America in 1584-1587. (This is the three hundred fiftieth anniversary.)

The first movements to make America Christian were colonizations: the Pilgrims in 1620, the Lutheran Swedes in Delaware in 1638, the Baptists in Rhode Island in 1639, the Friends in Pennsylvania in 1682. Continue and you will see a year's interesting sermons on missions.

One would also mention the labors of John Eliot (1649) whose memorial still stands in the Eliot Union Congregational Church of Lowell, Mass., and the work of David Brainard (1743) nearly one hundred years later. One must also mention the pioneer work of Wesley and Whitfield. The Lutherans and Moravians had already begun America's conquest for Christ in a thorough-going way as early as 1742.

From these beginnings Home Missions became an expanding movement of itinerants to win and retain homogeneous groups, English, French, Dutch, German, and Scandinavian, as they opened up the soil of the west. That movement, filled as it was with hardship and some natural perils and occasional opposition from the rougher element, was comparatively simple. That phase was practically completed in 1860.

After the war of 1861-1865, a whole new problem arose in the guidance of the freed Negroes and the Indians who had been herded on reservations. About 1890 a new phenomenon was observable. The old stocks, Pilgrim, Puritan, and Yankee, were now going and a new American type had definitely emerged. The America that had been proud, exclusive, assured, and unaware of the objectionable character of its manifest superiority, was suddenly becoming lonely and afraid. As it became a world power politically, its religious power began to recede. The growth of the cities, the rise of industrialism, and the influx of the European were paramount. Now had come a Catholic New England, a Hebrew New York City, a Negro South side of Chicago, a migrant population in the forests, grain fields and vineyards of the west. The rural church demanded a new technique. Denominationalism had begun to decay. There were large groups of isloated mountain peoples of whom we had but recently become aware. We began to glimpse new problems and to search for new methods. The old revival meeting, so able to stir America had sung its swan song. America had taken to wheels! wheels! and motors!

The frontier had not disappeared, but it had taken on a new character. Home Missions today is the most challenging field Christ has, the most terrifying. Its hope lies in the regnancy of Christ, in our own devotion, and in the tendency of society itself to break into units that can be handled. If we attempt it wholesale, we shall get nowhere. If we attack each separate unit as a project, we shall succeed. The character of our missionary statesmen today gives us the very greatest of hope.

THE CHILDREN

For those who make the children's sermon a part of every service the blackboard is the easiest thing to use for illustrations. Anyone can, with a circle and a few straight lines, have the ricksha of Japan, or the wheelbarrow of China. A small circle for a head, two slanting strokes for eyes, and two enlarging half circles on either side and one has a passable Buddha.

Practise until at one stroke one can draw the question mark or the listening ear, and then superimpose upon it the outline map of Africa. Many books are available on this development of presentation.

MONEY AND STEWARDSHIP

Sometime one must face the problem of money. The question of where the dollar goes is insistent. Roughly speaking probably here is a fair statement for the missionary dollar.

Twenty-two cents goes to the foreign field; 33 cents to the home field; 8 cents to ministers' pensions; 27 cents to Christian education; 3 cents to your own state and city; 4 cents to overhead; 3 cents to miscellaneous causes. If your own church has a different ratio, tell your people so. Many of them think it takes a dollar to send a dollar. Compare it with business statistics and methods of business houses.

Theodore Roosevelt, when he was Police Commissioner of New York City, conducted a Civil Service examination. He asked an Irish policeman what he would do to disperse a mob. "Sure and I'd pass the hat to take up a collection." Budgets must be interpreted. No one gives to a Board. They give to life. Preach some day on the question, "What would I do for the Lord's work if I had $1,000,000?" Parishioners were asked to send in answers. Here is one of the shortest submitted:

> "My wife and I have talked this over and are agreed that we should first pay our honest debts, less than $300. We should set aside $25,000 each to our three children, who do

not greatly need our aid, and $100,000 as a trust fund for ourselves. We should give our own local church $100,000 which is one full tithe of the whole, as an endowment. Note that we say give it, not pay it. We think of the tithe as excellent and desirable and have practised it for years, but we do not live in the Old Testament. We should then pay directly to the Foreign Society $50,000 as a perpetual trust fund, the principal of which would not be touched. We should deal similarly with the Home Board, the Publication Society, each of the Woman's Societies, the State Mission Society, the City Mission Society, the Ministers' Relief Fund, the nearest denominational college, and our denominational paper. There would still be left $224,700, which we should regard as a trust fund for the relief of anyone or any cause in an exigency. Our chief line of interest for years has been the development of the life of youth. We would hope to find several worthy young people whom we could give college training."

By all these means and others must our people be brought to give.

Dr. Edward Shillito has brilliantly revived for us a story of the English artist seated on a bluff overlooking the Strait of Dover. Wishing for a crayon to delineate the scene, he remembers that the soil beneath his feet, is the chalk from which crayons are made. In precisely like fashion the preacher will remember that the entire Christian movement is missionary, and can't be anything else but missionary. It is not isolated nor partial—it is all. In it you have the romance of preaching.